Model Railway Constructor
ANNUAL 1987
Edited by CHRIS LEIGH

Model Railway Constructor

Constructor

ANNUAL 1987

Edited by CHRIS LEIGH

LONDON

IAN ALLAN LTD

Contents

Cover:
Modern image 'somewhere in the Highlands'. Class 47 No 47712 *Lady Diana Spencer,* **a modified Hornby model, heads Lima Mk 3 stock. The scene was photographed outside with the natural sky as a background.** *Chris Leigh*

First published 1986

ISBN 0 7110 1634 8

Published by Ian Allan Ltd, Shepperton, Surrey; and printed by Ian Allan Printing Ltd at their works at Coombelands in Runnymede, England

D. G. Rowlands

Friends of the Trackbed

All photographs by the Author

Scenic garden railways up to 2½in gauge have featured in the model railway press right from its inception, being the subject of many thousands of words in hundreds of articles and a number of books; perhaps the best known being Ray Tustin's never surpassed (but sadly out of print) classic *Garden Railways* (Percival Marshall, 1949). For the present inquirer, let me recommend Don Neale's *Railways in the Garden* (Peco, 1978) and the excellent Handbook No 6 from the Gauge O Guild, *Garden Railways in All Scales* (1984).

Such writings usually dealt with construction methods in reasonable detail, and often had inspiring photos and helpful drawings, but few of them admitted to the pleasures and joys of the

garden railway. Indeed, at the risk of being contentious, I would suggest that many of the articles laid too much stress on the labours involved — foundations dug, so many tons of earth moved and concrete mixed, and vastly involved timetable operation making it all seem more like a prison sentence than enjoyment!

Even today, it is all taken so seriously. There is little mention of the joys of moving trains in a natural setting (which may be carefully cultivated or run wild according to taste); the smells

Below:
Three scales and three forms of propulsion on gauge 0 (32mm) track. Left to right: 16mm scale live steam *Rheidol*, 10mm scale battery operated Tralee & Dingle, 7mm scale two-rail electric standard gauge 0-6-0PT.
Author

of creosote, garden scents blending with hot
metal, steam oil and burning meths or (better
still) coal! The sounds of nature — birds and
insects, even of falling rain — with a train
working hard uphill and the rolling stock
clacking rhythmically over the rail joints. . . .
This, I venture to suggest, is what it is all about.
The difference one might say between a
draughtsman's general arrangement of an 'M7'
tank locomotive and the well known Cuneo
painting (Triang-Hornby catalogue No 13) complete with blooming willow-herb.

Having had an O gauge garden railway for
many years and tried electric, clockwork and
steam traction, including a long flirtation with
16mm narrow gauge, I have settled in my
dotage for a mix that enables me to masquerade
as Sir Josiah Stamp or W. H. Austen, as mood
dictates. The versatility of O gauge enables me
to run 7mm standard gauge in fine or coarse
scales (though *my* trackbed is really too
roughly laid for adequate fine-scale operation),
7-8mm vintage tinplate (with improved wheels),
10mm scale narrow gauge (3ft gauge types) and
16mm scale (2ft gauge types). I have eschewed
buildings, signalling and anything that would

look incongruous; and this has meant temper-
ing my love for overgrown trackbeds. For
whereas a narrow gauge tank locomotive
shouldering through the ground elder looks
right, it doesn't fit the image of a Gresley 'P2'
and a long string of wagons — though mossy
track is no impediment to heavily-leaded 7mm
locomotives. My clearances are to 16mm
maxima of course — two Archangel bogie
brake vans with side duckets are the widest
vehicles I am likely to want to pass, and for
height Dave Pinniger's cupola caboose (now
happily in the USA) provided that dimension
years ago.

We still read of those poor souls who give up
operating their lines when winter comes. The
winter months give a useful opportunity to
service rolling stock, it is true, but modern live
steam locomotives know no restraints due to
weather — be they internally or externally fired

Above:
Rural peace. A 7mm coarse scale '58XX' heads the pick-up goods. *Author*

— and there is nothing so flexible or utterly convenient as battery operation. I always keep a battery locomotive and a few trucks by the back door, ready for instant use: any time, any day. After-dark running also has a panache of its own that is best in autumn and spring, with occasional illumination by oil lamps (*not* flood-lighting).

Naturally, there is especial pleasure in the nice warm day — notably those 'soft', mellow days in autumn. There is nothing I like better than getting down to track maintenance (my line is at ground level) with the sun on my back and a steam locomotive sizzling away beside me at the head of a PW train carrying pliers, rail joiners, etc and that essential can of ale. My ears

are attuned to the birds and the insects, but more especially to the purring and hissing, and my nose is busy with the bouquet of hot metal and superheated steam oil.

Having reverted to some 2-rail electric running I found it necessary to replace a few rail-joiners and to solder up alternate ones as was my original practice. So there I was one spring day, having a marvellous time kneeling on a sorbo mat and replacing fishplates and plying soldering iron, while a simmering engine kept me company. It is only at such times, when close to the warm earth and enjoying the setting that one appreciates just how much a part of the environment a garden railway can become.

Many thousands of woodlice live beneath the trackbed. They are nocturnal in habit but scuttle for shelter when my packings, pokings and delvings disturb them. Much maligned by gardeners, they live on rotting leaves and fungi, not new plant shoots as is often alleged. I'm no entomologist but I believe there are about 40 different types. *Onicus* is the common one, and I always think in their later form those George England 0-4-0STs of the Festiniog looked rather like these armadillo-shaped bugs. They can get caught between the sleeper webbing and the rail on Peco track, and it is a friendly act to poke them free. This is no longer a problem for

Below:
In typically overgrown terrain, the Tralee and Dingle 2-6-0T (battery driven on Tri-ang chassis) heads a motley train of T&D stock. *Author*

me, however, for it is not only woodlice that can get trapped; thereby hangs a tale.

During the first 'Year of the Archangel *Brick*', which revolutionised propulsion on my AVR, I had left that docile but weighty pot-boiler trundling round the main circuit unattended while I nipped indoors. It was a lovely spring evening and the hedgehog family were about early, enjoying a snuffle in the grasses. Mrs Tiggy had indeed set off down the line, regardless of the warning signals. (Yes, I had them in those days!) Deciding to leave the trackbed, she got her toenail caught between rail and webbing. She promptly froze — her trapped foot stuck out incongruously behind and across the rail.

I Emerged from the back door, looked around for *Brick* and spotted the plodding engine tick-ticking along with the train about 2yd from the imprisoned Mrs Tiggy!

Luckily for her I had an instant reversion to schooldays and 'fielding practice'. I caught up a flower-pot and shied it at the wicket (ie *Brick*). The cab roof took the full impact, knocking the locomotive off the track and piling the train up in a heap of *flambé* stock. A bucket of water cured that, while I freed the hedgehog (quite oblivious of the trouble she had caused); then I could inspect the damage.

Thanks to the robust Archangel building, it was not too bad, though it proved easier to get a new cab roof from Stuart Browne than to try straightening the dented one! Otherwise, after straightening the buffer beam and chimney and touching up the paintwork there was no real harm done . . . though I had to scrap and

Above:
Vintage Archangel. In a scene of the 1970s an Archangel 'Rheidol' heads a VoR four-wheel brake third and a L&B bogie brake van. *Author*

Below:
A corner of the 7mm motive power depot with a two-rail 'Jubilee' (coarse scale) from Dawson components and a Bassett-Lowke 'Royal Scot' with improved wheels. At rear, a scratch-built 'Baby Scot' and a Bassett-Lowke live steam Mogul. *Author*

rebuild the open wagon that had caught a glancing blow from the flower pot and received most of the burning meths from the fuel tank.

Thereafter, I made sure that my cement-peat setting came up to rail bottom and so eliminated that gap between rail and webbing. A lot of friends wondered why I ran *Brick* without a cab roof for about six weeks that first season, and I blethered about it 'looking better like that'. Now they know the real reason!

Dead-nettles grow in profusion along the embankment in springtime. Gardeners seem to loathe them, but I like them and so do the bees which visit the purple flowers. They have a strongly minty smell and would probably flavour potatoes as well as does their relative, mint. Their oily seed growths are attractive to ants, who carry them off — what for, goodness knows. The leaf lacks hair and so is resistant to herbicidal sprays dispensed by rural councils and railway companies — it is a great plant for abandoned railways.

The embankment becomes a mass of dandelions in early summer turning their golden heads to the sun. These really are a liability of course, for their long roots can wreak havoc with the foundations of a miniature trackbed. But it would be a sorry time on the AVR without them and a shot of creosote after flowering takes care of their nuisance potential. They are so prolific that one need not fear killing them off. Of course, I leave them alone in the main part of the garden where they are succeeded by a riot of poppies in high summer.

It can take me three hours to cover 8yd of track. I could do it in about 10 minutes I suppose and go indoors to watch TV.

You may think I'm crazy, but that is what I built my garden railway for. Yes, I like running trains, and watching them, but best of all is just pottering about with a simmering steam locomotive close by, and with all the time in the world to enjoy it.

Crichel Down

Above:
Martin Goodall's Crichel Down, a minimum space Scalefour layout, was featured in *MRC*, January 1986.

Below:
The MWLR tram locomotive, a D&S kit, arrives at Crichel Down. The bridge is a Merit tunnel mouth.

Above:
A close-up of the detail around Crichel Down station building.

Above right:
General view of the yard area with *Gnat* passing the ground frame box on the left.

Below:
Crichel Down signalbox with working point rodding.

Right:
The 0-4-0 diesel heads a short freight into Crichel Down.

Above:
The *Gnat* brings in a mixed train, with the Highland Railway four-wheeler leading.   *Photographs: Len Weal*

A Midland Railway Signalbox

Above left:
Churchward Models produces this Midland Railway etched brass signalbox kit and two Great Western types in a variety of popular scales. This view shows the main assembly of the Midland Railway box.

Left and Top:
Two views of the completed Midland Railway signalbox.

Above:
Front elevation of the Midland Railway signalbox at Lazenby & Kirkoswald on the Settle-Carlisle line.
J. A. Wells

Right:
Dent Head, a smaller Midland signalbox, on 14 September 1967. *J. Scrace*

Paul Stoolman

The Growth of a Hobby - 1

Above:
Three of the five control panels on the Westport layout.

Railway modelling was not my first hobby. Photography was the 'in' thing when I was in my teens, and thanks to indulgent parents I was able to develop this quite fully, doing all my own developing, printing, enlarging etc, although the opportunities for doing so soon faded during World War 2.

I was in my thirties when the model railway bug took a hold, and although living in a flat of two small rooms at the time, the kitchen table was brought in to use, and some goods stock was constructed. One of the early Ratio kits was involved, made of ply and balsa wood, and very satisfactory this was too. It is apparent now that for fine detail in the smaller gauges you must go in for plastic or etched brass, but there is something basically very satisfying about working in wood, and I still retain the first L&Y fish van and GWR 'Toad' that were happily cut and stuck together on that kitchen table.

We moved to a house, and sons showing an interest gave me a good excuse to spend more money on railways, and soon every birthday and Christmas was the occasion for the purchase of further pieces of equipment. Very haphazard it was though, in those days and anything that took one's fancy was obtained. Next came a move to a larger house, and the decision to do something more permanent than laying tracks on the floor. The larger house was soon equipped with a workshop, and the desire for carpentry was expressed in a 6ft layout on legs in my sons' bedroom. 'Westfield' being the name of my house, the Westfield Railway came into being. The bug began to bite deeper and the 6ft by 4ft layout became the base for a terminus, with the line gradually extending all round the walls, with a lift-up section across the door. Gradually the bed space for my two sons grew smaller, but the domestic authority was persuaded that it was in all our best interests.

I was particularly interested in railway

16

Above:
Westport station approach with goods yard, signalbox and gantry.

operations at the time and fancied large and complicated control panels, so two boxes full of lots of lovely switches for the two main stations were built, intercommunicating with one another. These were on wheels so they could be pushed under the track when not in use. Developments eventually got to such a pitch, however, that even a well disposed wife began to look askance, and well justified complaints started to accumulate. Fortunately at this time an 18ft by 12ft hut in the garden, which had previously been used to store trunks belonging to my parents, became available. Electricity was

laid on, with heaters switchable from the kitchen. Insulation and double glazing was installed, and the Westfield Railway Mk 2 began to take shape.

At this time I came to the conclusion that a bit of anything and everything was really not good enough, and so I became more specialised. Since we lived in Western Region territory and had fond memories of holidays spent in the West Country, the decision was taken to model the GWR in the mid-1930s. Thus the Westfield Railway became the Great Westfield Railway. This involved some fascinating historical research, and a large library of GW books was rapidly built up.

With a good-sized room at my disposal, main line running was possible, and eventually a plan from the *Railway Modeller* was adopted. This was for a double track main line running round the walls with a spur off to hidden sidings at one end, whilst a large terminus named Westport, capable of holding eight-coach trains with a substantial goods yard and locomotive depot, was on a lower level at the other end. The approach road to this terminus runs just 3in under the main line along two sides of the hut, a long length of hidden track, which is not easy to get at when derailments occur. Thank goodness my couplings are based

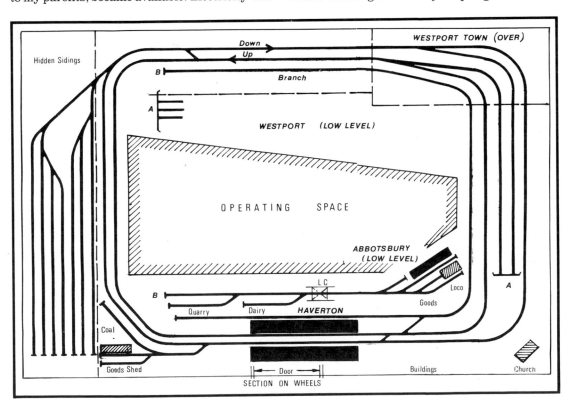

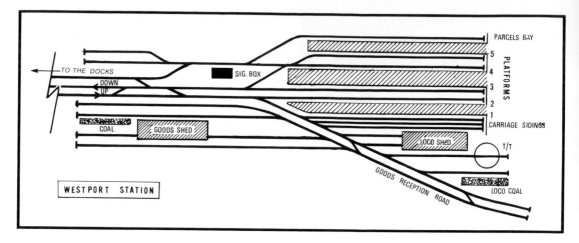

WESTPORT STATION

on the original Hornby-Dublo type, now supplied by Peco. These enable one to tip a piece of stock sideways to uncouple and remove from the track, which appears to be impossible with the ugly-looking tension-lock couplings now in general use on RTR stock.

The original plan incorporated a large locomotive depot on the side of the room not occupied by the terminus, but I changed this to a branch line. This departs from a bay in a through station named Haverton, situated on the main line. It goes right round the room, mostly under the main track, passes a quarry and a dairy and ends at the small country town of Abbotsbury. This gives me main line running from the terminus to the hidden sidings, with interconnecting branch line services.

I like to think of my layout in relation to the Weymouth line of the GWR, and trains run from the terminus Westport, to various destinations such as Paddington, Bristol, Exeter and the north. Locals stop at Haverton to connect with the 0-4-2T and auto-coach to Abbotsbury, whilst in the morning and evening rush hours, through trains consisting of a

Below:
Westport quarry.

Pannier and a 'B-set' run through from Westport to Abbotsbury. From Westport a line runs to the docks, which are not modelled due to lack of space, but there are ample storage tracks to stable boat trains and others, which run through from the main station.

I now have 21 locomotives consisting of just about every type that would have run on the line at the time, from 'Castles' to the little '1366' class dock tanks that operated the harbour line at Weymouth. Panniers predominate, of course, and I have permitted myself the luxury of a 'King', although this would never have appeared on a secondary line such as that to Weymouth. There is a Southern rake with an 'N1' Mogul, and a couple of through coaches from the LMS. The locomotives are all built from kits, though I regret to say that most were not built by me, basically through lack of time.

There is an eight-coach rake of Centenary stock (which sets my scene not earlier than 1935) with headboards lettered 'Channel Islands Boat Express', a rake of old Hornby Pullmans, and five other rakes of assorted toplights and clerestories. While the Centenary coaches, the Pullmans and the 'King' would not have been seen at Weymouth, they look so splendid that I could not resist them. I have about 140 assorted goods vehicles, and goods trains are made up using a pack of cards, with the destination decided by the card according to the type of vehicle and frequency with which it is likely to have moved. There are express freights and slow local pick-ups, coal trains coming in from Wales, mineral wagons to be loaded at the quarry siding, milk tanks for the dairy, and cattle wagons for the cattle dock at Abbotsbury.

The layout has five control panels. Two of these are at Westport, one for movements within the station and the other basically for down main line movements although this can be switched through to the station to help out when things get very busy there, which they do quite frequently. The third controls the hidden sidings and up main line movements, while the fourth is at Haverton and the fifth at Abbotsbury, looking after the branch line.

There are 10 main electrical sections on which cab control operates and any operator needing access to the main line can drive a train anywhere. Each of these sections has a warning light which lights up on each panel so that an operator does not switch into a section already occupied by someone else. There are a large number of sub-sections, particularly at Westport of course, and these took a lot of work and a lot of wire and switches to instal. Other circuits control point motors and the bell code system, each colour-coded. Although modern technology has made a lot of this unnecessary, I found installing the electrics enjoyable work, and whilst the circuits are basically simple, the uninitiated visitor never fails to be impressed when shown the back of one of the control panels. Even if I had the ability, I do not think I would want to instal relays etc for automatic operation, as the essence of the operation for me is driving the trains, and being the signalman.

Operation is by timetable covering a 24-hr sequence, carefully worked out by my eldest son, so that every single movement including shunting operations is scheduled. Each operator has a set of instructions relating to the

matters under his control, and when made up and ready, the train is offered to the next station up the line, using correct GWR bell codes. A green light is used, showing at both stations concerned, to indicate 'line clear', with a red light for 'train on line'.

I have thought of working to scaled up time, but things can sometimes get so hectic when there are five operators, that this idea was abandoned in favour of sequence working. After all, the purpose of any hobby is to provide relaxation, but even without the pressure of a time element, sometimes an operator can fall so much behind with his movements as to occasion caustic comments from another waiting to receive a train.

Maintenance can be a problem with a layout this size, but I hope that eventual retirement will provide the time to deal with this satisfactorily. Provided one runs trains fairly regularly, the track seems to keep itself quite clean, which is just as well considering the amount of hidden track involved.

It has taken me about 15 years to build this layout, but of course it is not finished. There are always improvements that can be made, such as making the signalling remotely-controlled instead of manual as at present, which would contribute significantly to operating pleasure, and generally improve the surroundings. Then there is the question of scratchbuilding, which in spite of the many excellent kits on the market would, I think, give one deep pleasure. There is always something to look forward to, which is what it is all about.

Below:
General view of Westport station.

David Monk-Steel, Paul W. Bartlett and Trevor Mann

BR Air-braked Coal Hopper Wagons

Drawings 4mm:1ft scale.

Railways were invented to carry coal and King Coal remains the staple freight traffic of BR. This article is about the two distinctive types of high capacity air-braked wagons which British Rail uses to carry much of its coal traffic nowadays. The first, and most important, are the merry-go-round (MGR) hoppers, the others are for domestic coal.

The Merry-go-Round Principle

The MGR principle was unveiled by G. Fiennes in *Modern Railways*, January 1963 when, as Chief Operating Officer BRB, he outlined proposals drastically to improve the means by which the railway handled coal. This concept has been so successful that one fifth of the BR-owned revenue earning fleet is today dedicated to MGR working. The scheme was originally conceived for the haulage of coal from pit to power station, but now embraces industrial, shipping and coke traffic.

However, the successful implementation of this concept may have appeared doubtful at that

Below:
1: On 19 October 1977 a train of MGR hoppers has delivered coal to Aberthaw power station and some of the wagons are on the weigh bridge. The internal cross bracing can be seen across the top of each wagon, and on many it is badly distorted by use. *BRB, Euston*

time for, if a Victorian coal baron had been carried by a time capsule to 1963, he would have found the transport scene at most of the collieries remarkably familiar. Simple wagons of between 13 and 21 tons capacity, which lacked continuous brake, were responsible for carrying nearly all of the production. Communications had made wagon control easier, but the fleet remained huge and was wastefully used. Much of it stood loaded throughout the summer as mobile stockpiles and, as minerals traffic was of low priority when in transit, these wagons could stand weeks in marshalling yards and colliery sidings waiting acceptance/redistribution, or just lost! So, productivity was very low.

Admittedly, during the war and postwar period, virtually the entire fleet of non-hoppered mineral wagons had been replaced by wagons of steel construction. Private ownership of the coal wagons had also ended, which allowed for some improvements in wagon productivity. But these new wagons did not lend themselves to easy means of mechanical unloading. They could be tippled or end tipped, but both of these means required each wagon to be uncoupled and handled individually. Some wagons of greater capacity were available, as discussed in *An Illustrated History of BR Wagons Vol 1*, Bartlett, Larkin, Mann, Silsbury and Ward (1985), (Oxford Publishing Co) but these were relatively few in number and until 1961 none of the higher capacity wagons had continuous brake.

Of course hopper wagons had also been used for carrying coal for many years. BR built more hopper wagons, at first by building 13- and 21-ton wagons of LNER designs. Later, a large 24½-ton capacity design was added to the fleet. Once again all of these wagons were unfitted, until a batch of vacuum braked 21-ton hoppers was introduced in 1958. Because hopper wagons required specialist unloading fixtures these wagons usually worked in circuits. The 24½-ton example was a successful attempt to improve the productivity of carrying coal to the power stations. Initially they were all branded for this type of traffic. The 21-ton hoppers were also used for traffic to the power stations and to docks for shipment coal. However, they had also always been used for domestic coal in the northeast. BR developed this idea by introducing Coal Concentration Depots in the main conurbations. Slowly all of the small coal depots working at almost every station were replaced by these depots, which proved very successful and continue in use. During the 1960s the vacuum-braked 21-ton hoppers which worked to them were branded HOUSE COAL CONCENTRATION along the hopper side, but they no longer have this distinctive lettering.

By this time there were also other schemes which had elements of MGR. The more significant were:

(a) Toton to Stonebridge Park power station with coal carried in bogie side-discharge hoppers;

(b) Iron ore from Tyne Dock to Consett in bogie side discharge hoppers;

(c) Iron ore from Glasgow General Terminus Quay to Ravenscraig in high capacity four-wheel hopper wagons;

(d) Coal from Kent collieries to Richborough power station in disc-braked 24½-ton hoppers;

(e) Block loads of 21-ton hopper wagons to Dalmarnock power station.

Thus, by 1963, none of these had all the necessary ingredients for true MGR working. However, as so many imaginative experiments had been going on with wagons for other traffics, the time seemed ripe for developments in coal carrying. The MGR development was the necessary radical departure from what was accepted, and seems to have rather surprised the National Coal Board who took some convincing before it was accepted.

The MGR principle was to introduce a 'bus stop' discipline into the working. The trains were to be continually on the move, even during loading and unloading, with no intermediate marshalling. The wagons were to be high capacity, air-braked, automatic discharge hoppers and a prototype was ready by April 1964. A model was on show a year earlier when, to reinforce the previous announcements with with new customer support, BR staged the 'Coal Handling Exhibition' at Marylebone. Journalists commented favourably, likening the new wagon to a contemporary French coal hopper, an impression no doubt influenced by the large extension canopy fitted.

During the time between the first

Above:

2: 350731, seen at Millerhill during August 1985, had been rebodied at Doncaster during the previous February. The additional horizontal row of bolts towards the top of the body side can be seen. The number panel is placed low on the side to avoid wear by the rubber wheels at some loading points. The wagon body is in natural steel finish with the framing in Railfreight red and all of the underframe is black. *Paul W. Bartlett*

announcements of the idea and the production of the prototypes there was considerable hard bargaining between all the parties concerned. The NCB was the main protagonist, arguing that as the productivity benefits lay with the railway, BR should pay for the new loading screens which would be required at the pits. Once the formal agreement was signed, on 7 January 1964, the NCB generating authorities and BR set about swiftly getting the equipment into use.

The large base-load power stations being constructed at that time were geared up to MGR operation almost from the start. Many of these were situated in the Trent Valley. Tests into High Marnam power station from local collieries in Nottinghamshire started in 1964. Scottish coal started moving in MGR wagons to the Cockenzie power station in 1966 from Monktonhall, Bilston Glen and Newbattle collieries locally, in Lothian Region. By the end of the 1960s very large quantities of coal were passing out of the Yorkshire, Nottinghamshire and Derbyshire Coalfields to the base-load power stations. Coal was also worked by MGR to Aberthaw cement works and power station in South Wales, but as the virtual closure of the entire South Wales coalfield was expected in the early 1970s the area has never been converted to MGR to anything like the same extent as others. Similarly developments have been slower in the northeast of England, however MGR working started to new staithes at South Shields towards the end of 1985.

Above:

3: The 1982 batch of Merry-go-Round hoppers were designed to operate at 60mph with modified running gear. The body has the same appearance as the rebodied HAAs. The air distributor can be seen on the further side of the platform behind the headstock. 368312 was at Tinsley in March 1984 when photographed and was painted similarly to *Photograph 2*. *Paul W. Bartlett*

The introduction of MGR required more than just new wagons. Trackside equipment and new track layouts were provided at power stations. High capacity bunkers and improved sidings were built at pit heads and BR improved junctions, resignalled lines and provided new maintenance facilities. The most spectacular civil engineering scheme associated with these improvements was the elimination of the flat crossing at Retford where frequent coal trains crossed the busy East Coast main line at 90deg on the level. A new station was built at low level and the east-west tracks dropped below the ECML under a new bridge. This arrangement also permitted the ECML line speed to be increased. Purpose-built maintenance depots were built at Knottingley, Worksop and Burton on Trent. Other wagon works such as Barry were equipped with the necessary specialised door operating mechanisms and also maintain the MGR fleets. At Knottingley a new locomotive depot was also provided.

Most power stations were equipped with unloading circles, fully signalled to enable two or three trains to be unloaded in rapid succession. These were supervised from control rooms in contact with BR signalboxes and power signalling was usually installed on lines leading to these locations to cater for intensive working.

In 1970 the Associated Portland Cement Manufacturers showed their faith in MGR when they opened their new works at Northfleet in Kent. Not only did they regularly receive trains of 43 loaded coal MGRs but they also had their own fleet of mini MGR wagons to bring Gypsum

from Mountfield in Sussex. These wagons, which now work for APCM in southeast Scotland, are basically a two-hopper version of the MGR wagons and were built by BREL Shildon. They had many components in common, including the same unloading mechanism. However, on comparing the two designs with a view to measuring the APCM hopper, the authors quickly realised that the designs differed in both most major dimensions and in many details. Bulk cement was also loaded on one of these circuits and, although this was not done with the train in motion, the BR locomotive remained attached. A power station type control room was provided.

Power stations also have the problem of flyash disposal. A fleet of air-braked enlarged 'Presflo' wagons operates between many of them and the brickfields near Peterborough where the flyash is used to infill old clay pits. Their working is interlinked with MGRs.

One of the prototype wagons had a canopy which increased its capacity to 32 tons. Unfortunately wagons so equipped fouled many older colliery loading screens so a decision was taken in 1967 to restrict these wagons to self-contained workings where their presence would not pose operating restrictions. The east Scotland working was considered suitable and the 145 wagons still retaining these canopies are concentrated there.

Wagons were originally classified as HOP AB or HOP 32 AB when fitted with a canopy. On TOPS they are classified HAA (Hopper, class A, Air-braked). Although this change was introduced in 1972 some wagons can still be seen bearing the pre-TOPS inscriptions.

Operation of MGR

As explained, ideally loading and unloading should take place while the train is on the move. This ideal is rarely achieved but some workings come very close. The MGR trains load under a rapid loading bunker at a colliery as the wagons are moved beneath it at very slow speed. These bunkers hold 2,000 tons of coal or more, so it is possible to load trains in quick succession. A typical train comprises 30-34 wagons so it may be seen that this large capacity bunker is essential. Trains are weighed electronically when on the move, and as soon as the guard has collected his documents from the colliery officials, will set off directly to the power station.

On arrival, the wagons are examined as the train draws slowly into the unloading station. The guard surrenders the documents and unloading commences. The wagons are weighed again. Then, as they pass the dis-

Figure 1—HAA.

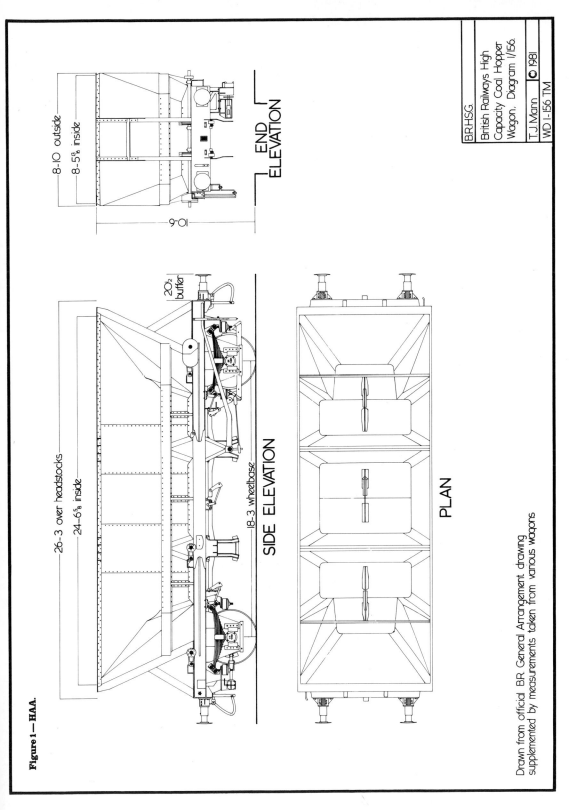

8-10 outside
8-5⅜ inside

9-6

END ELEVATION

2O₂ buffer

26-3 over headstocks
24-6⅝ inside

18-3 wheelbase

SIDE ELEVATION

PLAN

BR-HSG.
British Railways High Capacity Coal Hopper Wagon. Diagram 1/156.
T.J.Mann   © 1981
WD 1-156 TM

Drawn from official BR. General Arrangement drawing supplemented by measurements taken from various wagons

charge hopper, cams engage the operating levers on the wagons, unlocking the doors and opening them. When discharge is complete more cams shut the doors and replace the safety locks. The train is reweighed, then examined and any wagon that is seen to be defective or where a door has not properly closed or locked is labelled for repair. These are usually the only labels used on each wagon as the train is labelled as a whole and not individually. Some wagons have a permanent set number behind the label clip. The repair labels will be noted by the guard and reported to TOPS so that the train can be put in at a convenient repair point on the way back to a colliery and the defective wagons exchanged. It is essential that wagons are kept in full sets. Any wagon found to be too badly damaged to leave a power station will be detached there and placed in a dedicated cripple siding for attention by mobile repair gangs.

This method of working is the ideal, but some collieries are not equipped with rapid loading bunkers and, at some, the NCB locomotive will move MGR wagons underneath colliery screens to load, and BR locomotives will be attached in an exchange siding. Alternatively, the BR locomotive will place the wagons alongside a concrete apron where mechanical shovels will load a few wagons at a time, from a coal stack. The train will pull up two or three times during the loading sequence. This is called 'Pad Loading'. There are also restrictions on the numbers of wagons that can be safely handled on different routes, so some trains may run in two portions to an intermediate siding where

they will be joined for the onward journey.

At some loading and unloading points wagon moving devices are used instead of locomotives. One type uses a 'beetle' or rope hauled wagon and others use electrically-driven rubber tyred wheels to propel the wagons along. This latter method leaves distinctive tyre marks about halfway up the wagon side and wagons in regular traffic to places using this method are easily identified. The loading and unloading sequences must be carried out at a steady slow pace. Locomotives in use on MGR trains are usually fitted with an electronic device which the driver can operate which ensures that the train moves at a constant speed irrespective of load or gradient. The following classes are so fitted:

Brush Class 47/0 & 47/3;
English Electric Class 20;
BR Class 56;
BR/Ruston Class 58;
BRCW Class 26;
BRCW Class 33/2.

Not all locomotives of each of these classes are fitted. At one time the English Electric Class 50s were so fitted but they had this removed some years ago.

To assist the driver during movement, special signals are provided. These are operated by the man in charge of the bunker or hopper. These signals were first used at hump shunting yards and are often known as 'Toton' signals because of their first use there. The 'Stop' aspect can also be applied by the guard who is stationed near the loading point and watches for any incident which endangers the train.

Trains are run in sets, the size of which is determined by the locomotive power available, the characteristics of the line and terminals, and the flow of coal. Class 47 locomotives working to the Trent-side power stations are authorised 30 wagons, whereas a Class 56 may take 34. A Class 56 can take 45 wagons between Barrow Hill (Staveley) and Didcot. Trains from North Nottinghamshire to the APCM works at Northfleet are of 43 wagons with either a Class 56 or 47. Although not fitted with slow speed control other locomotives such as Class 37 and 45 may be used but the loading may be reduced and they are used only to locations where wagon moving devices are available. Similarly other classes, such as the now withdrawn electric Class 76s and West Coast main line electrics could be used for a main haul between marshalling yards. In Scotland trains of 28 canopied wagons are normally hauled by pairs of Class 20 or 26 locomotives. When propelling is a feature of the journey an air-piped brakevan is provided and, until recently, all trains worked by Class 20 were obliged to convey a brakevan as well. Brakevans for MGR trains are modified to clear the unloading equipment and the top step board is cut back. These vans are illustrated by photographs and a drawing in *Model Railway Constructor*, May 1983, pp279-283.

Finally, before discussing the wagons themselves it is worth mentioning that a common use for these wagons during the 1960s was as barrier wagons for block trains of oil tank wagons.

The wagons: Construction and Design

The prototype wagons were ordered from the BR development unit at Darlington and delivered in 1964. B350000 appeared in April without a canopy and B350001 followed in December with one. They were ordered to lot No 3495 and heralded the northeast's long association with the fleet, all but 160 being built at Shildon. Ashford in Kent built the others as lot No 3558, numbered B351682-351841. Details of the building programme are given in *Table 1*, as can be seen a maximum of 10,701 has been built, but at 1 January 1983 the total was 10,608, about 10 were withdrawn each year because of accident damage, etc.

The design has remained remarkably standard during the 18 years of its production. With the exceptions mentioned later the entire fleet is covered by diagram 1/156. This has been superseded by the more detailed TOPS design codes tabulated in *Table 2*.

As shown in *Fig 1* and *Photograph 2* the wagons are constructed of steel, consisting of a stout underframe to which a supporting framework of steel sections is attached and in which the galvanised hopper body sits. The underframe and framework are welded. The body is riveted using modern cold rivets which make panel replacement fairly simple.

The hopper body consists of three steep hopper chambers sealed with wide double doors at the bottom. The steep sides ensure that coal drops through rapidly and the wide doors swing clear to give a large aperture. The doors are worked from a cross rod which is attached to the levers which engage the trackside equipment. On one side a pair of gear wheels are interposed to ensure that the rod only turns in the correct direction. The discharge mechanism is quite efficient, however, problems have been encountered because the coal is usually washed and damp when loaded and could freeze to the doors. To help overcome this problem an anti-freeze spray is applied at some collieries during freezing weather. Accidental door open-

Above:

5: 351598 is an example of a standard top skip HAA. It is in original condition and, although the number panel has been re-applied, the outline of the HOP 32AB black lettering can just be seen above it. Photographed at Millerhill in August 1985. *Paul W. Bartlett*

ing is a very serious danger, so safety catches are fitted which must engage before the wagon is loaded. Tell-tale flags are built into the mechanism and part of the lever system is painted a bright colour to aid identification. The door catches themselves are operated by a series of cranks and levers which also engage lineside equipment. If the doors cannot be closed properly after discharge, the wagon is permitted to travel to a repair point, the doors being designed to stay clear of the loading gauge.

The wagons are equipped with the BR standard air-brake system and in common with Freightliners are the only air-braked vehicles still required to operate with a separate reservoir pipe coupled throughout. This ensures great braking efficiency. The air-brake pipe and reservoir pipe are arranged to couple crosswise below the coupling, unlike all other air-braked vehicles which have the air-brake reservoir pipes mounted on the same side of the coupling hook, one above the other. This required special short-length pipes. The brake linkage applies disc brakes on to the wheels on opposite corners of the wagon. The hand brake linkage, similar in many respects to the old LNER design, operates shoe clasp brakes to the treads of the wheels in opposite corners, that is at the other end of the axle. Some wagons have disc pads mounted on the wheel centres. Westinghouse equipment is used on most of the fleet, but some vehicles in the lot ranges 3844-3887 have Davies & Metcalfe equipment. To permit a higher axleload the engineer insisted on 3ft 7in diameter wheels. Oleo hydraulic buffers, Timken roller bearings and single-link suspension are standard to the fleet.

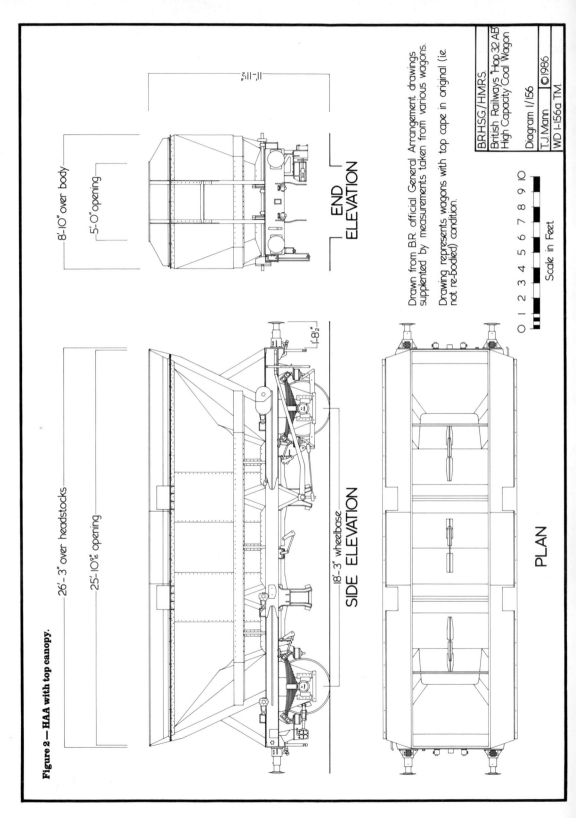

Figure 2 — HAA with top canopy.

26' - 3" over headstocks

25' - 10¹⁵⁄₁₆" opening

18' - 3" wheelbase

1' - 8½"

SIDE ELEVATION

8' - 10" over body

5' - 0" opening

11' - 11½"

END ELEVATION

PLAN

Drawn from B.R. official General Arrangement drawings supplemented by measurements taken from various wagons.

Drawing represents wagons with top cape in original (i.e. not re-bodied) condition.

0 1 2 3 4 5 6 7 8 9 10

Scale in Feet

BRHSG/HMRS.
British Railways 'hop.32 AB
High Capacity Coal Wagon

Diagram 1/156

T.J Mann   ©1986
WD 1-156a TM.

Tare weights vary depending on type of body, and whether a canopy is carried or not. Lot No 3645 with a light alloy body has a tare about 1¾ tons lighter. A canopy adds about ¾ ton. Wagons which have been rebodied are about 1 tonne heavier, as heavier section of 5mm is used for the new body panels, in contrast to the ⁵/₃₂in section originally used.

The variations from standard and modifications include:

1 The canopy, which was an integral part of the original design. Unfortunately only a limited number of colliery screens could handle the additional height, so as already mentioned, the wagons were transferred to Scotland. They were fitted to about 150 Scottish wagons, 145 of which survive, see *Fig 2* and *Photographs 5, 6, 7* and *8*. Apart from the odd exception, Nos 356155, 356200, and 357916 it is doubtful if any other wagons numbered above 354300 were ever fitted with canopies and wagons up to this number will lose the bolt holes when being rebodied. Other examples of the canopied wagons are 350941, 351010, 351094, 351117-9, 351223-5, 351562-4, 352705-12, 352730-3, 352740-6, 354262-7 and 354280-3.

2 The rebodying programme. The original design featured four cross struts fixed across the top of the body side to stiffen the flat side panels (as can be seen in *Photograph 8*). Unfortunately the weight of coal dropping into the wagon from the loading bunkers soon bent these bars, which eventually broke away. Once the support had gone the sides became vulnerable to distortion. To overcome this problem the body was given an additional stiffening plate riveted along the whole length, see *Photograph 2* and *Colour C*. This redesigned arrangement was applied to new construction from 359447 onwards, the four cross struts being dispensed with at the same time as seen on *Photograph 4*. All rebodying of existing wagons after 1977 incorporated this style of body, although wagons rebodied prior to 1977 were given like for like replacement.

The revised body can be recognised from the side by an additional line of rivets along the body, and the removal of the eight short stiffeners on the lip of the body. The bolt holes for the canopy were discontinued some time earlier. Rebodying takes place at Doncaster Works using a kit of parts fabricated in the workshops. The body is assembled as a free standing unit using huck-bolt rivets, a hydraulically applied cold rivet similar in principle to pop-rivets.

Above:

6: As can be seen in this photograph of 352742 the wagons of experimental lot No 3645 of diagram 1/157 are easily recognised as the body is of welded, not bolted, construction. That the bodies were of a light alloy can most easily be seen by the tare of 12·200Kg, which was about 1¾ tons less than the others. Although not perpetuated this experiment appears to have been successful. The wagon was in original condition with the early HOP 32AB lettering showing at Millerhill in August 1985. *Paul W. Bartlett*

There is one other difference applied to late, and rebodied wagons which affects the shield to the door operating lever gear wheels. On the original wagons the shield was provided with rounded ends, later and repaired vehicles are fitted with square ended shields, as *Photograph 5* and *6*.

3 The uprating of the design to run at 60mph when empty. Although not always done at the same time, most wagons are being upgraded to operate at 60mph empty, but the modification is not obvious to external examination and reference to TOPS is needed to distinguish these vehicles.

Although the fleet is largely similar as might be expected with such a large number of vehicles, there have been a handful of experiments. The more significant were:

(a) Six wagons, Nos 352741 to 352746 of lot No 3645, diagram 1/157, were fitted with hopper panels of aluminium, instead of steel, see *Photograph 6*. Despite the saving of about 1¾ tons this was not used again.

(b) One at least, B352728, had a Metalife treated body with anodic coating, No 1000, which was coded E/DN/59, see *Photograph 7*.

(c) In 1977 there were a number of suspension experiments carried out on various vehicles, 359570 was selected to be the HAA representative and was fitted with advanced parabolic taperleaf suspension. The vehicle was usually found in RTC Derby but at the end of 1985 it was condemned at Doncaster Works and awaiting dismantling for spare parts.

(d) Also in 1977 experiments were carried

Above:

7: Another experimental body treatment was applied to 352728, a top skip HAA. It had a Metalife treated anodic coating No 1000, once again from new with the original lettering still visible. The body ends and some panels on the sides appear to have deteriorated. This wagon was also at Millerhill in August 1985. *Paul W. Bartlett*

out with air-operated doors. Wagon 359571, in *Photograph 4* was fitted with three sets of air engines which actuated the door mechanism under air pressure from either the reservoir pipe or from a shore supply. The door catches were retained. The fitting of pipes and tubes was very experimental, being held to the framing by tape. The operation of the air valves was performed by cams which were compatible with the standard door opening gear in power stations. The effort required to operate the cams was far less than required manually and no doubt simplified trackside operation was envisaged. A full description was in *Modern Railways*, April 1979. It would appear that the air doors were not worthwhile, which was unfortunate as the idea would have allowed greater flexibility in the use of converted HAAs. Originally the vehicle was integrated into the whole fleet but, by mid 1984, it was branded RBA. By early 1985 its number was given the departmental prefix ADC and like 359570 it was condemned at Doncaster by the year end.

The HDAs

One of the snags was the restricted speed, which was not a problem where journeys were short and largely on lines reserved mainly for MGR trains. But, with the coming of long haul trains from the East Midlands and the Northeast to Northfleet or Didcot in the south the slow maximum speed of 45mph of the HAAs became an operating inconvenience. There was also a need to put smaller quantities than a train load on 60mph Speedlink services. To overcome these problems 460 wagons, with TOPS code HDA, were delivered to lot No 4008 in 1982 with

improved braking and suspension to permit them to run at 60mph when loaded or empty, see *Fig 3* and *Photograph 3*. The services they currently operate are from North Derbyshire and North Nottinghamshire to Didcot, Northfleet and Westbury, from Whitehaven to Fiddlers Ferry, near Warrington and to Claydon Cement Works, Suffolk from Bolsover, this latter on Speedlink services.

These wagons are standard with the rest of the MGR fleet, except that the air-brake cylinders are more robust and occupy more space under the headstock. To accommodate this the distributor is mounted on the top of the wagon floor. The suspension is slightly different and the air-brake pipes are mounted in the normal Speedlink style on the right-hand side of the draw hook. These wagons normally operate two-piped but, when marshalled in a Speedlink train they may run single-piped. The wagons feature the later style body. They were also fitted with passenger/goods changeover lever but, in practice, this was found to be an unnecessary complication and was disconnected, the equipment being sealed in 'goods' timings. The original TOPS design code was HD001A but as the changeover lever was disconnected the wagons have been progressively reclassified HD001B.

Liveries of HAA and HDA

The first wagons were turned out in unpainted galvanised steel finish, with the framing and gear shields freight brown, although there were instances of these shields being black or in primer. The underframes and running gear were black laquer. The numbers and inscriptions were painted on in black and the first two wagons were inscribed 'High Capacity Coal Wagon' in the centre of the side panel. The code was HOP 32 AB for wagons with a canopy and HOP AB for those without, see *Photographs 6* and *7* and *Colour photograph A*.

From about 1974 the TOPS code HAA started to replace HOP AB and was normally applied in white on a black panel. Wagons became discoloured through use and a feature of these vehicles was the twin lines of tyre marks along the flat body sides, left by the wagon moving equipment at some terminals. This operation gradually wore away the lettering in its original position and the number was often stencilled back on in white directly over but not always synchronised with the original black painted number. Later the numbers were applied slightly lower down to avoid being worn away and were usually positioned on a black panel, see *Photographs 2* and *3* and *Colour B*.

Table 1 — Merry-go-Round Hoppers

Running numbers	Quantity	Diagram No	Lot No	Builder	Year
B350000-350001	2	1/156	3495	Darlington	1964
B350002-251681	1,680	1/156	pt 3528	Shildon	1964/65
B351682-351841	160	1/156	3558	Ashford	1965/66
B351843-351881	40	1/156	pt 3528	Shildon	1965
B351883-352693	811	1/156	3574	Shildon	1966/67
B352694-352740	47	1/156	3575	Shildon	1966/67
B352747-354246	1,500	1/156	3646	Shildon	1967/68
B354247-254296	50	1/156	3647	Shildon	1967/68
B354297-355044	748	1/156	pt 3670	Shildon	1968/69
B355045-355344	300	1/156	3688	Shildon	1969
B355345-355396	52	1/156	pt 3670	Shildon	1969/70
B355297-355796	400	1/156	3699	Shildon	1969/70
355797-356246	450	1/156	3720	Shildon	1970
356247-356746	500	1/156	3751	Shildon	1971
356747-357246	500	1/156	3788	Shildon	1972
357247-257396	150	1/156	3815	Shildon	1973/74
357397-358246	850	1/156	3844	Shildon	1974/75
358247-358496	250	1/156	3864	Shildon	1975
358497-358856	360	1/156	3869	Shildon	1975
358857-359176	320	1/156	3882	Shildon	1976
359177-359569	393	1/156	3887	Shildon	1976/77
359570	1	1/156	3887	Shildon	1977
359571	1	1/156	3887	Shildon	1977
B352741-352746	6	1/157	3645	Shildon	1967
365000-365299	300	HA002C	3978	Shildon	1980
365300-365499	200	HA002C	3984	Shildon	1980/81
365500-366129	630	HA002C	3997	Shildon	1981/82
368000-368459	460	HD001A	4008	Shildon	1982
Total	10,961				

During 1979 the freight livery was altered to flame red and grey and the MGR fleet received their own version of this as they passed through shops. Nearly all of the wagons with the new style body have the revised scheme and the old style bodies also receive it if they get an intermediate repair which does not include rebodying. With the new scheme, bodies remain as either natural galvanised finish or aluminium painted and the framing supporting the hopper is flame red, see *Colour photograph C.* The shields were usually painted black, like the underframes, but some have had flame red shields. There is also some variation as to what constitutes body framing.

One notable variation existed on the experimental air-door wagon where the later livery has been applied but the wagon floor, air cylinders, valves and above-floor operating equipment are in flame red, as is the stiffening ridge around the top of the wagon, see *Photograph 4.*

Above:

8: The top view of a number of top-skip HAAs can be seen in this view of Millerhill during July 1984. The internal cross bracing can be seen; it is noticeable that the pair of inner ones are nearly as high as the skip itself whereas the outer pair are simple L-angle as carried on the more common HAAs. The wagon in the foreground is 352725. The wagons without top skips behind it are not HAA but the APCM owned version of them, as mentioned in the text. *Paul W. Bartlett*

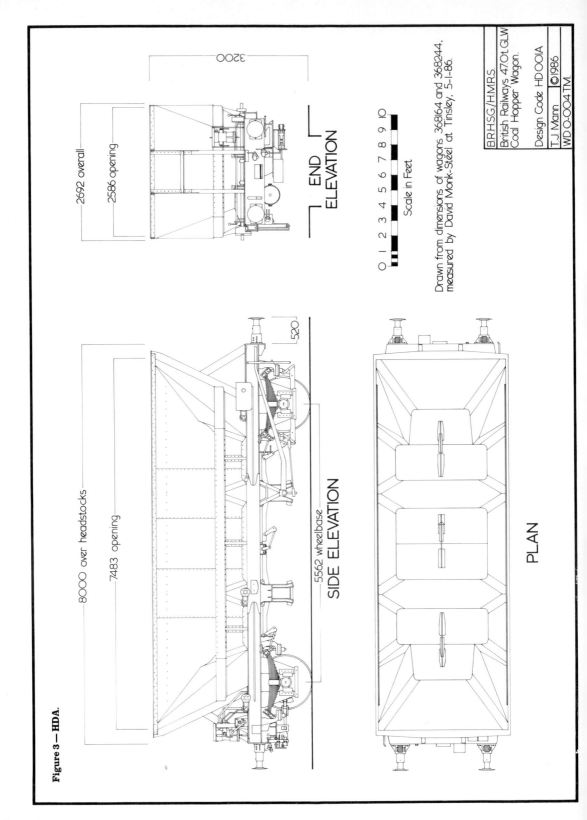

Figure 3 — HDA.

END ELEVATION

SIDE ELEVATION

PLAN

3200

2692 overall

2586 opening

8000 over headstocks

7483 opening

5562 wheelbase

520

0 1 2 3 4 5 6 7 8 9 10
Scale in Feet

Drawn from dimensions of wagons 368164 and 368244, measured by David Monk-Steel at Tinsley, 5-1-86.

BRHSG/HMRS
British Railways 47.0t GLW
Coal Hopper Wagon.
Design Code HDOO1A
T.J. Mann   ©1986
WDO-OO4TM

All new liveried wagons have their numbers, TOPS code and weight inscriptions in white on black panels. Where buffers have been replaced these are often left in primer or undercoat and green, yellow and red have been noted. The exposed lever of the door catch mechanism is often given a bright distinctive colour to aid operating staff to see if the catches are engaged.

Air-braked domestic Hopper Wagon

Although the MGR wagons were amongst the first wagons of the modern air-braked fleet, 12 years were to pass before a more conventional air-braked coal hopper was introduced. This new design was necessary because large quantities of coal continued to be worked to unloading points where provision of the expensive MGR unloading facilities was unjustifiable. Many docks, coal concentration depots and factories were able to unload conventional hoppers, so these new hoppers worked in block trains to some of these and they could also work individually in Speedlink trains.

A prototype No 360000 was built at Shildon to lot No 3881, and lot No 3885 quickly followed in 1976. By mid-1979 1,998 had been built at Shildon, this order should have been for 2,000 wagons but two sets of underframes were used to construct prototype scrap carrying wagons as illustrated in Bartlett *et al* (1985), p74. These wagons are initially known by their TOPS code HBA.

As can be seen in *Fig 4, Photographs 9-12* and *Colour D* the wagons are strongly made of steel and have a conventional hopper body arrangement with large flat sides. They are 24ft 4in over headstocks with a 15ft wheelbase, the body being 8ft 9in wide and 6ft 7¾in above the top of the solebar. There are two hopper doors with each opening between the wheels. The body is

Above:

9: 360199 is an example of the domestic coal HBAs. When seen at West Thurrock during October 1982 it was in original condition with a bauxite coloured body and solebar and conventional springs. This example is an early wagon built during 1976 at Shildon with the ladder on the centre line of the body and fine stays near each corner linking the top of the solebar with the main cross strut on the end. What appears to be its diagram number, HBA 001 is painted on the solebar above the left-hand hopper door release lever. *Paul W. Bartlett*

supported by a flying buttress arrangement, there are two at the ends and three on the sides. Early examples also had a fine stay near each corner, see *Photograph 9*. These early wagons also had the ladder on the centre line and grab handles on the upper part of the end buttresses. The change in the ladder and other arrangements happens between No 360216 and No 360242. Thus, unlike the MGRs where the hopper sits in a nest of supports, the hopper body and its supports are integrated together.

The solebar is largely parallel and 10in deep. It curves down to the deeper 12in headstocks

Table 2 — TOPS design codes

Code	Description
HA001A	MGR hopper with canopy, 55mph empty, steel body
HA001B	MGR hopper with canopy, 55mph empty, light alloy body
HA001C	as HA001A, permitted 60mph empty, steel body
HA001D	as HA001B, permitted 60mph empty, light alloy body
HA002A	MGR hopper without canopy, 55mph empty
HA002B	MGR hopper without canopy, 55mph empty, redesigned body and air operated doors
HA002C	as HA002A but with later style body from new, 55mph empty
HA002D	as HA002C but with experimental parabolic taperleaf suspension
HA002E	HA002A wagons rebodied to HA002C standard, 55mph
HA002F	HA002A wagons permitted 60mph empty
HA002H	HA002C wagons permitted 60mph empty
HA002K	HA002E wagons permitted 60mph empty

All types are permitted to run at 45mph in all loaded conditions.

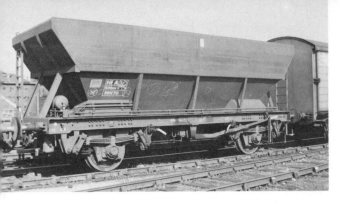

Above:

10: Another hopper retaining its original bauxite livery is 361170 at Norwich during September 1983. It was resprung using Bruninghaus springs during February of that year and the central B of the TOPS code has been modified to an E by simply painting over with a strip of black paint. The code on the solebar continued to be HBA. In comparison with the previous photograph the other side and end of the wagon is shown, with the air-brake cylinder on the end platform and the pipe runs. The latter is repositioned to the left-hand side and there is no stay at the corner. *Paul W. Bartlett*

over the outer suspension brackets. In this they differ from many contemporary air-brake designs which have solebars of more complex shape. However, it still means that the suspension brackets are of different design either side of the wheel and there is also a weighing unit for the self-adjusting brake, as seen in the nearest bracket of *Photograph 10*. The brake lever is conventional in that the brake guide is to the outside of the wheel centre line and it pivots on the centre line. Once again this is different from other air brake wagons which usually have short brake levers. The explanation of this arrangement is that it was probably designed to avoid the hopper door release levers. The brakes are discs bearing on the wheel centres.

The suspension is the other feature which has changed the appearance of these wagons. The design was introduced with BR friction link suspension; 13 leaf springs were necessary to carry the 32.5-tonne payload and tare of about 13.2 tonne. This meant that the wagon had a maximum speed of 60mph. With this suspension the wagons were given the design code HB001A. Several wagons had experimental suspension; the ones we know of were 360285 which had Gloucester floating pedestal units, (this was the last HBA wagon and by the end of 1985 it was condemned), 360781 which had an experimental Taperlite suspension, 360955 had Gloucester floating axle, 361776 had Gloucester springs, 361797 had British Steel Friction control pedestal and 361798 friction control taper leaf. We are unsure when these were

equipped like this, but most were probably from new.

None of these experiments were successful as several of them were still limited to a maximum speed of 60mph. In 1979 it was decided to alter the suspension so that the wagons were capable of working in the fastest Speedlink trains at 75mph. As an experiment Nos 361782-361796 and 361799 were fitted with experimental Bruninghaus suspension in 1978. This was immediately successful and from 361800 all were fitted with Bruninghaus springs from new. These may have been different to the experiment as 361785, for example, was resprung with new Bruninghaus springs in June 1979. These continued to be TOPS code HBA, like all of the earlier wagons until, towards the end of 1981 it was decided to differentiate these wagons by using the TOPS code HEA. At the same time it was decided to convert all of the earlier wagons to having the same type of suspension. *Photographs 10* and *11* and *Colour D* have this. This policy of conversion took until 1985 to complete.

Liveries of HBA and HEA

The first livery for these wagons was bauxite for the body and solebar, the remainder of the running gear was black. The only lettering was the usual number panel which was near the left-hand side on the sloped-in part and wheelbase and other markings on the solebar. *Photographs 9* and *10* show this livery.

Towards the end of the delivery of these wagons, the new Railfreight liveries were introduced. As an experiment 361552, built in July 1978, had Railfreight red for the entire end of the body and also for the flat part of the side. The sloped lower part of the side was in Railfreight grey. The solebar, all running gear

Above right:

A: B350314 is a representative of the first production batch of Merry-go-Round hoppers built in 1965. When photographed passing Cardiff General in June 1970 it was in original condition with a natural finish galvanised body and bauxite supports. The number panel appears to have been repainted recently and is in black applied directly to the body side. The significance of the PFA lettering is not known. The HOP AB code and B prefixing the number are notable. *Paul W. Bartlett*

Below right:

B: Another wagon in original condition but built 10 years later is 358294 which was photographed at Toton in September 1978. The livery is similar but the number panel is black with white lettering and the TOPS code HAA has replaced the code name. The other side of the wagon is shown, with only a single V hanger and one tell tale on the door gear. The side shows signs of rubbing by the type of unloading facility which uses rubber tyres to draw the wagon through. *Paul W. Bartlett*

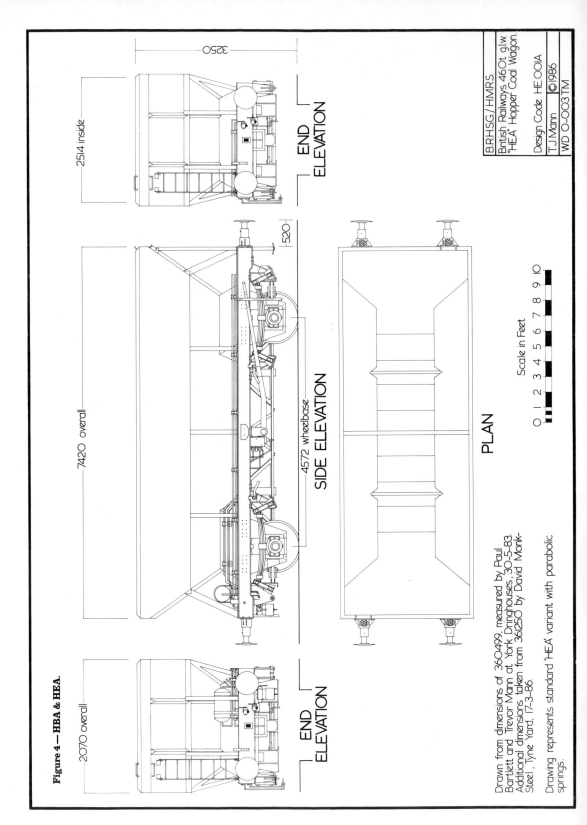

Figure 4 — HBA & HEA.

END ELEVATION

SIDE ELEVATION

PLAN

3250

2514 inside

7420 overall

4572 wheelbase

520

2070 overall

BRHSG/HMRS
British Railways 46·0t. g.l.w.
"HEA" Hopper Coal Wagon.
Design Code HE·OOIA
T.J.Mann   ©1986
WD O·OO3TM

Scale in Feet
0 1 2 3 4 5 6 7 8 9 10

Drawn from dimensions of 36·0499, measured by Paul
Bartlett and Trevor Mann at York Dringhouses, 30-5-83.
Additional dimensions taken from 36l25O by David Monk-
Steel, Tyne Yard, 17-3-86.

Drawing represents standard 'HEA' variant with parabolic
springs.

34

and top of the end platform was black. In addition to the usual number panel there was a large neat 'Railfreight' with a BR double arrow symbol alongside. These were positioned together towards the right-hand side of the flat side of the body and were surrounded by individual boxes. In April 1979 the new Railfreight liveries became standard and were to be applied when wagons received Main works, intermediate or general repairs. We believe the last few wagons received the new livery from new. We cannot be sure but 361992 was in a neat red and grey when seen during 1979 appearing to have been like this from new whereas 361991 was in a non-standard red and grey when seen during 1985, having been repainted recently so it may originally have been bauxite.

The specified arrangement of the red and grey was to have been to have all the upper part of the body in red and all of the lower part of both the ends and sides in grey. The ladder was white and the solebar and all running gear black. The 'Railfreight' and BR symbol were large and on the flat sides towards the left-hand side and within boxes. *Photograph 11* is like this.

Perhaps fortunately for the modeller, the instructions on lettering were often misunderstood and great variety was soon to be seen, for some wagons were repainted within two years of being built and repainted wagons were becoming a common sight by the end of 1979; though many continued in bauxite at the end of 1985. *Colour photograph D* shows a common variant with the Railfreight lettering too small and high up. This example had the boxes in solid lines but dashed lines could also be used, as they could for the larger lettering style. Early on, some of the wagons with either large or small lettering did not have the surrounding boxes at all, whilst others had cruder hand painted lettering or stencilled lettering with a different face style. One other variant was that some of the number panels had a black ground. Finally, in early 1985, 150 wagons were pooled for use in Scotland and a St Andrews cross label identified these, as in *Colour photograph D*.

Modelling Possibilities

In the article we have discussed the use of the MGRs in detail. As they normally work in block trains large numbers would be required. However, fewer could be used if a small colliery was being modelled of the type where only a few wagons were loaded at a time. Photographs of this type of operation are to be found in books which specialise in industrial railways such as *Steam in the Coalfields*, (Heavyside, G. T. (1977), David & Charles). Perhaps modelling

Above:
11: Another resprung wagon and therefore also coded as HEA is represented by 360359 at York Dringhouse Yard during December 1983. It was converted in July 1983 but, by then, it had already been repainted into Railfreight red and grey so the B of the code has been crudely altered to an E. *Paul W. Bartlett*

the HDAs would be preferred as they could be used in small numbers in Speedlink trains. The problem of needing large numbers of these wagons is partly solved because, in 4mm scale, Hornby make a reasonably accurate model and in 2mm scale Graham Farish and MiniTrix make suitable models. We hope that this article allows for some alterations to be made to these to make their appearance more prototypical.

At present the IIBA would have to be made from scratch, a difficult job in any scale with the various unusual fittings, most of which are not available to modellers. This is an unfortuate omission from the modeller's fleet. Such a numerous class which can be used both individually and in block trains, and which also had two distinct liveries, seems to be a good candidate for a kit or proprietary model.

Finally, we would like to thank F. Seeds and E. Straw for facilities and help, R. Wallace and D. Larkin for some of the data and S. J. Slinn for printing the photographs.

Overleaf:
Top:
C: Displaying the later livery, which is now being applied to all of these wagons as they receive general repairs, is 365410, which was built in 1980 and photographed at Workington in April 1981. Railfreight red is used for the body supports and the position of the number panel has altered again. Differences from the earlier wagons are the additional horizontal row of bolts high up on the body side and the squarer profile tell tale to the door operating gear. *Paul W. Bartlett*

Bottom:
D: The other type of hopper discussed in our article is represented by 360642. When seen at Radyr in April 1985 it was carrying phurnacite from the works at Aberaman to Mossend. The St Andrew's cross indicated it was part of a Scottish pool; this symbol was a new feature on these wagons at that time. The lettering panel shows that the TOPS code HEA had been altered from HBA when the wagon was resprung, so this was more recent than the repainting, the wagon would have been maroon when newly built. *Paul W. Bartlett*

Paul Stoolman

The Growth of a Hobby   2

All photographs by the Author

Above:
Meths-fired pot-boiler based on the Lynton & Barnstaple *Taw* and built by Archangel, on the Westfield Light Railway. D. B. Pinniger

Whilst deriving great enjoyment from the electric remote control of trains and much pleasure from creating a piece of countryside in miniature, I have always been fascinated by the idea of live steam models. For a long time, however, this only seemed possible in the passenger-carrying gauges, which of course required much space usually only provided by club grounds, and much expense, unless one had expertise and equipment to build for oneself.

Advertisements by a firm called Archangel Models had intrigued me for some time, and then a new world seemed to open up when Jack Wheldon's articles in the model railway press appeared, and I learnt that a good deal of activity seemed to be taking place with 16mm scale narrow gauge. This offered small narrow

gauge prototypes running on gauge O track, but since the scale is substantial, the engines were a really good size. If they were main line models they would in fact approach passenger hauling possibilities, since the scale used would be roughly equivalent to gauge 3 in standard gauge track size.

Here was the answer for which I was looking — live steam at a price I could afford, which could be run in the space at my disposal in my garden. Furthermore, the usual rural surroundings and rather happy-go-lucky atmosphere of prototype narrow gauge practice could readily be recreated in a garden setting, without any great need for buildings and a scale

background which is usual in the smaller sizes. What one is in fact doing is driving an engine instead of operating a layout, and exchanging the role of General Manager of a system for that of driver and fireman, with a touch of mechanical engineering and track laying thrown in.

The layout of your garden will decide where the track will go, and in my case a path alongside a shrub border was the obvious choice. Since a continuous circuit is very

Above:
L&BR 2-6-2T *Taw* and train approaching Crocus Valley halt.

Below:
Shrublands station.

desirable so that one can enjoy an uninterrupted run without having to chase after the engine, I installed a loop at each end with double track alongside the shrubbery.

Assuming the ground is fairly level, a decision must then be made as to the height. Ground level tracks look very nice with trains wending their way through flower beds or rockeries etc, but in my case, since I have now got to the age where bending is no longer easily accomplished, I was quite certain that my track must be elevated, preferably to waist height. Since live steamers require close personal contact especially when raising steam to start with, this decision has not been regretted.

Above:
The enlarged Archangel 'Sgt Murphy' named *Hercules*.

Another question concerns track levels along the run, and unless you are going to use exclusively radio control, then gradients are not really desirable, unless you are prepared to accompany the locomotive on its journey, so that the regulator can be adjusted as required. I carefully used a spirit level when installing my track bed, but even so I ended up with one or two

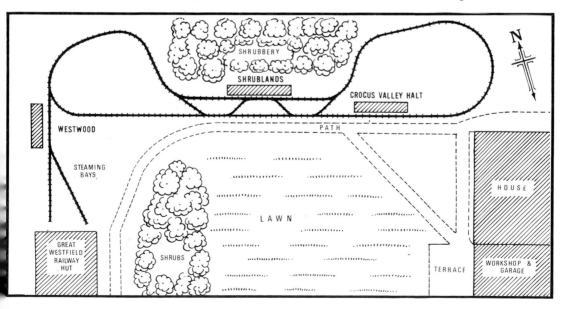

Above:
Taw heads a sizeable train of VoR stock into Shrublands. *D. B. Pinniger*

Above right:
Coal-fired Bagnall 0-4-0T of the Cliffe Hill Mineral Railway named Jack.

Right:
Paul Stoolman prepares his coal-fired Jack for the road. *D. B. Pinniger*

slight gradients, although not enough to cause any real problems.

Having made these decisions and drawn up a scale plan to determine the amount of wood required, I went off to my local timber merchant and ordered the necessary number of pegs for the uprights, which are 2in by 2in posts sharpened to a point so that they can be driven in to the ground with a sledgehammer. These were set 4ft apart for the straight lengths and 2ft apart for the curves, and to the top of each were screwed two lengths of 2in by 1in strip, horizontally, for the track bed to rest on.

The track bed itself is of 1in thick planks, 5in wide for the single track at the end loops, and 10in wide for the double track portion. The 10in planking proved to be a mistake for warping has caused the edges to curl upwards in places, and two strips of 5in would have been better. I asked the supplier whether these could be creosoted to prevent rotting, and found that these days the messy business of creosoting has been replaced by a process known as tanalising, where the wood is put into a tank and subjected to special pressure treatment.

Since I have 210ft of track, several months of labour then went by installing the track base, and this work is best done in the autumn or spring when the ground is softer. Although most locomotives in this scale are designed to negotiate 3ft radius curves, a larger curve looks better if you have the space, and mine are 6ft. A 6ft length of string attached to a stake acted as a compass to get the curves right. I spent the best part of one autumn, winter and spring building the track and then I was asked what would happen if there was a derailment and the train fell off! Since a drop of some 2½ft on to a gravel path would not be likely to do a valuable model much good, I then had to spend several more months putting up a fence on both sides, consisting of 3in brackets at 12in intervals with wire mesh stretched between.

At last I was ready to run and then came the pleasant task of deciding what it should be. I had already acquired a little Mamod which I had been running on its own track in the garage, and this was much improved by the installation of a gas burner from Merlin Models. After some teething troubles promptly put rightly by Mamod themselves, this has proved to be a good

runner giving about 10 minutes run on one filling of the boiler and gas tank, but I was now after something better.

I had always felt that if I was going to go in for live steam, then I was going to do it properly, and to me that meant shovelling coal into a firebox, getting to know how to use a blower and generally being an engineman. So having managed to save up enough money, I bought Archangel's model *Jack*, a small coal-fired quarry type locomotive. This engine has a cross-head pump to keep the boiler full, so apart from the blower there was another control involved, the bypass valve to regulate the flow of water from the tanks. The fuel used is known as 'anthracite peas', and as I have some friends who use this in their household boiler, and who kindly offered to keep me supplied, this was another problem solved.

I soon found that there is indeed an art involved in driving a coal-fired engine, and *Jack* demands constant attention when running, to regulate the speed, keep the fire stoked and drawing properly and control the water supply — all great fun. There is also a good deal of preparation involved, filling the boiler and water tanks in the first place, making sure the lubricator is full of special steam oil, generally oiling the motion and ensuring that one has a supply of meths-soaked coal to start the fire,

with the aid of an electric blower. Afterwards there is the firebox to be raked out and cleaned, the smokebox to be emptied of ash and the tubes brushed through, not to mention a general clean up and polish.

However, I felt that something a little more sedate was also called for, when the mood is for a little leisurely running. The answer here was a pot boiler, where all that you have to do having prepared the engine, is to light the fire and then stand back and watch progress round the track. So I then bought *Hercules* which is an enlarged two-cylinder version of the well known *Sgt Murphy*, meths fired, and this is a most well-behaved and satisfactory engine. Subsequently I have acquired *Taw* which is a beautiful model of one of those splendid engines that used to run on the Lynton and Barnstaple line in Devonshire. *Taw* is radio controlled, which opens up another world of possibilities, and I now have a locomotive stud for all occasions. The only thing missing, as far as I can see, is a simple battery-operated job for those occasions when one wants to get something running with the minimum of delay.

Rolling stock is taken care of by a rake of Vale of Rheidol coaches made up from Archangel kits, and I am currently constructing a goods train. This has been started with the Tenmille kits of Lynton & Barnstaple stock, and I shall soon have to look around to see what else is available.

Having got my track and rolling stock I became aware of the Association of 16mm Narrow Gauge Modellers which I joined and now enjoy receiving their news-sheet. Having made contact with other enthusiasts in my area, we spend some very pleasant afternoons visiting each other's establishments and running our trains on their tracks, whilst receiving some useful hints and tips, good entertainment and pleasant company. This has shown me that it is not enough to just have a circuit of track, for when friends come to visit there is a need for extra sidings or steaming bays. Thus whilst one train is running on the main line, others can be raising steam, out of the way. So it was back to the wood merchant.

After some 30 years of railway modelling indoors and out, what is there left to do? Well I can think of several projects which I never had time for, but my main ambition now is to set up a proper metal-working workshop and build my own locomotives.

To this end I have booked myself on to a Model Engineering course at my local Technical College, where I hope I shall be able to acquire some of the necessary expertise. Also I might go back to my first hobby, photography, and start to take some decent pictures of the model railways I have built.

In conclusion I would mention that when one approaches retirement as I am, people tend to say: 'What are you going to do with yourself?' Well, I certainly have the answer to that one!

Left:
The radio-controlled Lynton & Barnstaple 2-6-2T *Taw*.

Below:
Double-track straight down the length of the garden.

Chris Leigh

A Canadian Station from Humbrol Beginnings

Everyone loves a bargain. Railway modellers often seem quite happy to buy something just because it is at a 'bargain' price, even if they have no immediate use for it. My local model shop had on special offer a number of the Humbrol Euromod building kits. These are imported from Sweden and consist of precut and punched wood parts plus plastic doors and window frames and card roof components. At £1 each, I reasoned that they would be worth buying for the plastic mouldings alone, even if (somewhat unlikely) I threw the rest away. I splashed out and bought a station building and a small goods shed and consigned them to an ever-growing pile of unbuilt models 'which might get built when I retire'.

There they remained for some months. At Easter 1985 our Fraser Canyon HO scale Canadian layout was exhibited at the Wembley exhibition. Several modellers, speaking from their own experience, warned us that life would fall very flat after our appearance at IMREX. We became acutely aware of the prospect that we would be bored with the layout. After all, IMREX is surely the peak of any layout's career, anything else is bound to be an anticlimax.

So it was that in the exhibition bar over a couple of pints of the beer which supposedly enables you to do the impossible, we began to dream up a way of extending the layout. This is not really the place to describe the layout extension, but suffice to say that we have added a second, scenic, viewing side to the layout without compromising the Fraser Canyon section in any way. This new scenic section allowed stabling for another three trains and also gave us room for a small wayside station. Inevitably, we decided that the new section should be ready by a certain exhibition deadline,

Below:
The box-lid illustration of the Humbrol/Euromod Swedish station.

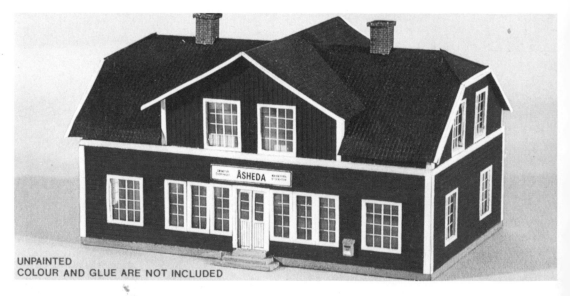

UNPAINTED
COLOUR AND GLUE ARE NOT INCLUDED

in this case our own club show in January 1986. That deadline is just four weeks away as this is being written!

Unlike the 'Canyon' itself, the new section does not feature major scenic work in the form of vast areas of rock face. In view of this, our deadline could be met if we minimised all the other scenic work as well. I already had a Campbell Models water tank which had been Canadianised and was awaiting some useful employment. While browsing through my

Above:

The former Canadian Pacific Railway station on the transcontinental main line at Chase in British Columbia in 1977. Features of this building were incorporated into the Humbrol model in order to make it appear more Canadian. *K. R. Willows*

Below:

The main alterations on the platform side can be seen in this view of the partly-built model. A window on either side of the main door has been omitted, the upper floor windows have been moved much higher, and the eaves extended to form a canopy. *Chris Leigh*

photographs I noticed a marked similarity between the freight depot at Banff, Alberta, and the box illustration of the Euromod kit. It is no coincidence that Swedish and Western Canadian structures are similar. Climatic conditions are much the same in both countries, and both have plentiful timber for building materials. The goods shed was duly assembled, with a new platform built from balsa to match the one at Banff. The only other alteration was to replace the printed card roof supplied in the kit with sections of Wills corrugated iron sheeting.

The resultant goods shed looked quite pleasing, so I studied the station building with a view to giving it similar treatment. The Canadian railway companies each had their own distinctive styles of architecture for small stations, indeed, they each had a number of standard designs to suit various locations. Since we operate trains from most of the major western railways on the Fraser Canyon it was felt that we should go for a typical-looking station rather than modelling a specific example. Here, the Euromod kit came into its own.

Careful examination of available photographs, plus the books *Railway Stations of Western Canada* and *Canadian National's Western Depots*, revealed that one feature was common to the vast majority of smaller timber stations. The eaves were extended to form an awning on the platform side, and sometimes all the way round the building. Windows were used quite sparingly, and there was usually a rail- or sleeper-level board walk on the platform side.

Examination of the Euromod kit showed that the elevations were all quite flat, but that the large gap between the ground floor windows and those on the upper floor, could be utilised to extend the eaves to form a canopy. All that was required was to recut the window apertures in the upper floor gable section slightly higher, as

Above:
Duncan, BC, now a 'heritage building' protected from demolition shows the way eaves were extended to form an awning. *Chris Leigh*

Below:
Port Alberni, BC, shows similarities to Duncan, with the hip roof, extended eaves and bay widow overlooking the platform. This view dates from the early 1900s. The station has long gone, and been replaced by a freight depot built of modern corrugated sheets.
Chris Leigh collection

will be seen by comparing the illustrations of the original and converted models.

Other alterations were minimal and consisted of not utilising the windows on either side of the main door on the platform side, and also one end window. The latter was to be concealed behind a lean-to extension which did not form part of the kit. This provides for a section house or baggage room according to one's particular requirements. The walls were cut from card, faced with $^1/_{32}$in balsa and scribed to match the planking on the main structure. Doors were made up from balsa and a spare window moulding was incorporated in one wall. The roof was of Wills corrugated iron and the interior has Campbell barrels and Ratio pallets scattered about.

The walls of the main structure were assembled according to the kit instructions and a $^1/_{16}$in thick balsa platform was added in place of the steps supplied in the kit. The building was glazed and an upper floor of card was fitted. The black roofing card supplied with the kit was utilised to provide 'walls' or light barriers inside the building, and greaseproof paper fitted behind the glazing partially obscures some windows.

The main departure from the kit is the roof, which I made from good quality card. The front section was cut to fit around the gable and to give the required eaves overhang to form the awning. The underside of the awning section was faced with $^1/_{32}$in thick balsa and scribed with planking. The roof section was then glued in place and the supporting braces for the awning installed from strips of $^1/_{16}$in balsa. These are very plain and simple diagonal braces.

The rear roof sections and the gable pieces were also cut to shape from card and installed on the building at this stage. Note how the awning is extended at one end and has a hip-roof section carried round the end wall. This is quite usual, and provides covered access for persons arriving by road to step straight under the awning without too much exposure to the elements.

Roof coverings in western Canada include materials such as tar-paper shingles, and corrugated iron. A more expensive method, usually confined to better quality dwellings is to use 'shakes'. These are split red cedar sections produced in a similar fashion to slates and used in the same way. The shakes weather to a greenish grey colour. I had 'shake-roofed' a small waiting shelter and been pleased with the result so I decided to use the same method on the station.

I began by glueing a thin strip of $^1/_{32}$in balsa along the lower edge of each roof section in order to set the shakes off at the right angle. The shakes themselves are pieces of $^1/_{32}$in balsa sheet measuring some 6mm along the grain, by 4mm across it. The size does not need to be too accurate, since a nice random appearance is required. Using Pac or Loctite Clear adhesive, the shakes were laid just like slates, remembering to get the staggered 'bonding' of the rows correct.

Before fitting each shake it was pressed firmly with the craft knife handle to reduce the thickness by about half, and a fine gap was left between adjacent shakes. This job is long and fairly tedious, being best tackled in short

Above:
Rural timber station and section house at Ladysmith, BC, in 1981. *Chris Leigh*

Below:
The converted Humbrol/Euromod station showing the effectiveness of the new roof covering and also the weathering of roof and walls. The baggage trolley is from Grandt Line and the lantern man is 'Wireless Willie' by the Mikros Corporation. *Chris Leigh*

sessions of about 2 hours each. I guess the roof covering must have involved at least a dozen evening's work, and a rough estimate indicates that around 2,000 individual shakes were used.

The station buildings of Canadian National and BC Rail are generally painted in various pastel shades. Those of Canadian Pacific (very few small timber wayside stations are now left) were a 'rust' red colour and I am not sure whether this was painted, or was the natural finish of treated and weathered red cedar. Anyway, I opted for the CP style, with a well worn look characteristic of such structures in the late steam and early diesel era. The walls and window frames were given one coat of diluted Humbrol matt rust coloured paint in order to achieve the desired effect. This gives a good grain impression on the plastic mouldings.

The roof was similarly brushed with dilute matt grey, green, black and brown, with rust colour dominant on the corrugated iron section. Before painting, the roof ridges were 'dressed' with a strip of tissue paper. The chimney and TV aerial came with the kit, the baggage trolley is by Grandt Line, and the working lantern man is 'Wireless Willie' by the Mikros Corporation. The resultant station has been named Fraser Mills (no connection with the real place of that name), and is set in the foothills of the Rocky Mountains.

Tisdunn

Above:
A general view of the detailed scenic work on Graeme Schrouder's Tisdunn OO gauge layout which was described in the August 1985 *MRC*. *Len Weal*

Below:
The '2251' class 0-6-0 departs from Tisdunn with a parcels train. Tisdunn forms part of the popular Branch Line Album exhibition layout. *Len Weal*

Above:
An ex-Rhymney Railway 0-6-2T passes behind the wagon repair company's locomotive shed.

Below:
Railcar No 22 leaves Tisdunn halt. In the foreground is the wagon works headshunt.

Left:

An Atlas Alco RS-3 finished in British Columbia Railway colours, crosses a delicate timber trestle with a work train. White water is essential to this tumbling creek, but note also the debris deposited by flood water. *Chris Leigh*

Below:

An NWSL Shay featured on the same diorama in a view which shows clearly the sparkling clear resin-cast water. The rocks are from plaster castings. *Chris Leigh*

Above right:

With the casting resin still wet the lifeboat model is placed in position, to be held firm once the resin sets. Plastic models should be protected by covering the hull with clear adhesive tape or the resin may melt the surface.

Centre right:

The long curing time of the resin allows plenty of time to work on the embedding of the wool. Used in this way, one is trying, without benefit of any movement, to create the impression of a fast-moving scene which lasts for only a few seconds. The colour illustrations on this spread should be compared when judging the success of this particular application of the technique.

Below right:

Perhaps the ultimate application of the white water technique. Note that the 'wave' effect is rather more convincing than the mass of spray. In a scene that would be an interesting scenic feature of a TT gauge layout, 37ft 6in 'Rother' class lifeboat *RNLB J. Reginald Corah* launches from her slipway. *Chris Leigh*

Chris Leigh

Scenic Suggestion – Model Lifeboats

Most railway modellers have at least a passing interest in other forms of transport, and most British people have a great regard for the work of the lifeboatmen. Many of us only ever see a lifeboat during our seaside holidays, and few will have actually seen one in action. Model railway layouts are often built to represent coastal locations and are inspired by fondly remembered seaside vacations, so what more natural than to add a lifeboat to that harbour scene on the layout?

Modellers working in TT, 3mm:1ft scale are lucky, for the Royal National Lifeboat Institution markets a small range of lifeboat model kits in this scale. Those working in other scales can readily size up or down the measurements from the RNLI kits, carving their hull from a balsa block and fitting a superstructure made from styrene sheet.

The present RNLI fleet comprises some 260 vessels ranging from 17ft 6in inflatables for inshore work, up to the 70ft long 'Clyde' class. For scenic purposes one of the intermediate types will be more interesting, especially if it can be depicted 'in action', such as during launching.

The conventional fleet is quite well covered by the RNLI range of kits, which are made of cast white metal and should therefore provide no problems to a railway modeller. Two obsolete types are featured, a 35ft self-righting vessel suited to the 1930s-1950s period, and a pulling and sailing boat which suits the late 19th/early 20th century. The last vessel of this type survived at Whitby until 1957. The kit features the horse-drawn carriage from which the vessel is launched and it therefore makes a fine period-piece to place in the street or on the sea front of the layout.

The next, more modern type is the 37ft 'Oakley' class self-righting vessel introduced in the late 1950s and still widely used. This vessel can be launched down a slipway, by tractor and carriage, or by skids laid on a beach. Some years ago Frog produced a plastic kit for an 'Oakley' in about 7mm:1ft scale. Despite the very obvious

Below:
Two of the RNLI kits used together in correct fashion. The 37ft 'Oakley' class lifeboat of late 1950s vintage, rides on the Case tractor and trailer. Many 'Oakleys' remain in service and are still launched in this way.

size discrepancy, I featured one on my old St Ives layout in a dramatic and quite incorrect slipway launch. St Ives is one of many locations where the lifeboat is launched from a carriage drawn by a specially waterproofed tractor. A typical Case tractor and trailer with caterpillar tracks, is among the RNLI kits and enables the 'Oakley' to be displayed in classic setting.

Finally, in the RNLI range are two more modern vessels, both types which are kept afloat on station and can therefore be correctly depicted afloat in a harbour scene. The 44ft 'Waveney' is based on an American hull design, while the 52ft 'Arun' represents the largest vessel in the model range and one of the largest and fastest vessels in the current RNLI fleet. The 'Arun' model has a one-piece cast metal hull and the amount of metal in this alone more than justifies the very reasonable price tag.

The RNLI kits are not 'shake the box' models and care and time spent in construction will be well rewarded — particularly in obtaining a good fit of the hull and deck parts. Handrail stanchions can be replaced with brass wire for better appearance, the handrails and looped grab lines on the hull sides being best made up from 5amp fuse wire fixed with Superglue.

I did a conversion job on one of the kits illustrated here. The 37ft 6in 'Rother' class lifeboat is a development of the earlier 'Oakley' to enable the fitting of radar and modernised self-righting arrangements. The conventional 'Oakley' can now be fitted with radar thanks to the light weight of modern radar sets. The 'Rother' has a smoothed 'Oakley' hull and an enlarged cabin.

I used the RNLI 'Oakley' kit, building the hull and decks and then filing off unwanted details. The cabin was built up from styrene sheet and most of the 'Oakley' details were used. The radar

Above:
A 'Rother' class lifeboat converted from the RNLI 'Oakley' kit, a straightforward job well within the capacity of any railway kit-basher.

Below:
A model lifeboat house, loosely based on the one at Swanage, showing a typical extension to accommodate a larger modern lifeboat. Wills building materials were used, together with Formcraft window mouldings.

was cut from the 'Oakley' mast and a new mast arrangement made up from brass rod. The 'Rother' is unique in the current fleet in being the only type which can be launched by all four methods: kept afloat, launched from slipway or carriage, or manhandled across a beach on skids.

It is worth noting that there have been a number of changes in colour schemes over the years. The RNLI kits have coloured box illustrations to give guidance, but the 'Oakley', at least, has undergone three subtle changes in

Above:
Largest of the RNLI model kits is the 52ft 'Arun' class, seen here in partly assembled state awaiting final paintig and fitting of handrails. The 'Arun' lifeboat is kept afloat on station.

Below:
Standing at the top of her slipway is the 37ft 6in 'Rother' class lifeboat *RNLB J. Reginald Corah* on station at Swanage. *Chris Leigh*

its lifetime. The original scheme had the well known navy blue hull, with white below the waterline, and the decks, upper hull sides and cabin in light grey. In the early 1970s the grey cabin gave way to the now standard bright orange — for obvious reasons. Incidentally, lifeboats carry a standard flashing blue light similar to that on land-based emergency vehicles. Finally, and probably only since the early 1980s, the hull sides have been all navy

blue above the waterline, with non-slip deck areas in a matt dark grey finish.

Equally important in correctly depicting the lifeboat scene are the shore facilities, which will invariably include a lifeboat house, even if the current vessel is kept afloat. The model lifeboat house illustrated is based on that at Swanage and shows how the building was modernised and enlarged to accommodate the present vessel. I used Wills moulded plastic building materials to represent the stone walls and tiled roof, with Formcraft window frames. The folding doors are balsa and card.

The slipway extends into the building, the short gap where the footpath runs in front of the doors, being bridged by a pair of removable wooden rails. The slipway is supported on concrete blocks which diminish in height as they get closer to the water. These were shaped from balsa blocks, while the slipway rails were from some 'I' section stripwood readily available from model shops. Note the rollers in the centre of the slipway, on which the keel of the lifeboat runs. On the model these were sections of ⅛in diameter aluminium tube, as used by aero modellers.

Finally, for modellers whose interest in this subject may have been aroused, the RNLI produces a number of useful books obtainable through local RNLI branches or from its head office at Poole. Among these is *A Guide to Lifeboat Stations and Museums* which lists details of vessel and visiting facilities for all the stations in the UK and Eire.

Overcombe recalled

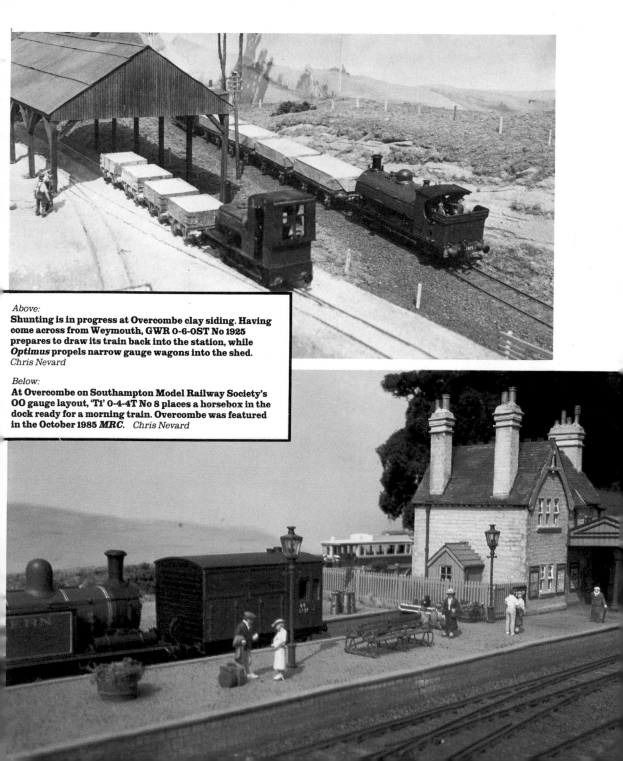

Above:
Shunting is in progress at Overcombe clay siding. Having come across from Weymouth, GWR 0-6-0ST No 1925 prepares to draw its train back into the station, while *Optimus* propels narrow gauge wagons into the shed.
Chris Nevard

Below:
At Overcombe on Southampton Model Railway Society's OO gauge layout, 'T1' 0-4-4T No 8 places a horsebox in the dock ready for a morning train. Overcombe was featured in the October 1985 *MRC*.   *Chris Nevard*

Above:
Sheltering in the cool of the clay shed, the photographer captures 'Jubilee' No 642 coming under the bridge with a midday local to Bournemouth West. *Chris Nevard*

Right:
The tide is out as 4-4-0 No 567 rumbles over the river bridge with a down goods. *Chris Nevard*

Above:
The approach to Overcombe, an SR branch terminus situated on the Dorset Coast. *Chris Nevard*

Eric Taylor

Kit or Scratch-built?

Do other modellers, I wonder find themselves in this position from time to time? Are you:

In a place where locomotive kits are not available? (There may be the odd one, but I have not discovered it yet.)

Keen enough to send overseas for kits and necessary spares?

Patient enough to wait some 10-12 weeks for them to arrive?

Careful as possible in deciding on what is needed as 'extras' to a kit?

Do you make good notes of what has been ordered? One will have done a lot of sleeping, as well as diversions to other jobs before the package gets here (with a nasty demand from the Customs Department for more of that 'folding stuff' that used to buy so much more.) By the arrival, one will have long since forgotten what was ordered.

There are probably several other factors involved, but the foregoing are enough to set the scene.

Two or three years ago, I ordered a body kit of a 'King' class locomotive by a well known manufacturer in the UK to fit on to my scratchbuilt chassis. All the parts, plus the 'extras' were there and the finished model turned out quite well. So free running, in fact, that it rolled off a folded newspaper on the kitchen table and nose-dived over the edge. After many 'blue' words plus the new buffer beam and straightened frame and paint touch-

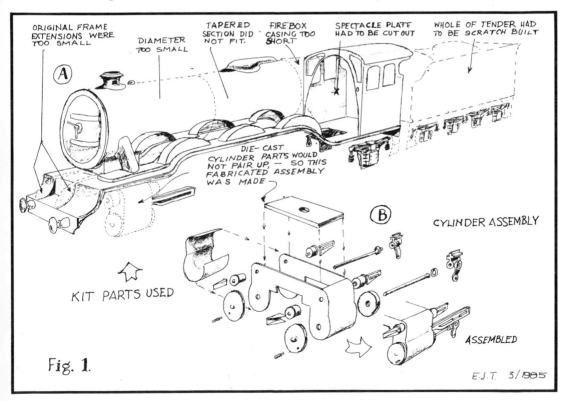

Fig. 1.

ORIGINAL FRAME
EXTENSIONS WERE
TOO SMALL

DIAMETER
TOO SMALL

TAPERED
SECTION DID
NOT FIT.

FIRE BOX
CASING TOO
SHORT

SPECTACLE PLATE
HAD TO BE CUT OUT

WHOLE OF TENDER HAD
TO BE SCRATCH BUILT

DIE-CAST
CYLINDER PARTS WOULD
NOT PAIR UP, — SO THIS
FABRICATED ASSEMBLY
WAS MADE

KIT PARTS USED

CYLINDER ASSEMBLY

ASSEMBLED

E.J.T. 3/1985

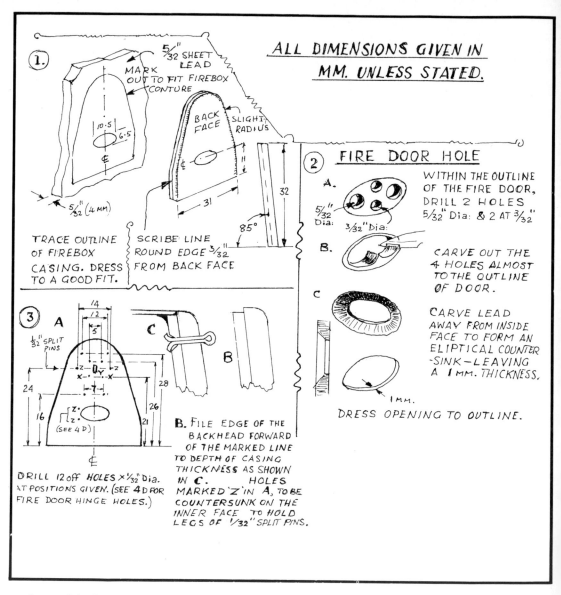

① $\frac{5}{32}$" SHEET LEAD

MARK OUT TO FIT FIREBOX CONTURE

BACK FACE   SLIGHT RADIUS

10·5   6·5

$\frac{5}{32}$" (4 MM)

31   32   85°

TRACE OUTLINE OF FIREBOX CASING. DRESS TO A GOOD FIT.

SCRIBE LINE ROUND EDGE $\frac{3}{32}$" FROM BACK FACE

② FIRE DOOR HOLE

A.

$\frac{5}{32}$" Dia: $\frac{3}{32}$" Dia:

B.

C

WITHIN THE OUTLINE OF THE FIRE DOOR, DRILL 2 HOLES $\frac{5}{32}$" Dia: & 2 AT $\frac{3}{32}$"

CARVE OUT THE 4 HOLES ALMOST TO THE OUTLINE OF DOOR.

CARVE LEAD AWAY FROM INSIDE FACE TO FORM AN ELIPTICAL COUNTER-SINK — LEAVING A 1 MM. THICKNESS.

1 MM.

DRESS OPENING TO OUTLINE.

③ A

14   12   5

$\frac{1}{32}$" SPLIT PINS

24   16

(SEE 4 D)

C   B

Z   Y   Z   X   X   Z

28   26   21

DRILL 12 off HOLES × $\frac{1}{32}$" Dia. AT POSITIONS GIVEN. (SEE 4 D FOR FIRE DOOR HINGE HOLES.)

B. FILE EDGE OF THE BACKHEAD FORWARD OF THE MARKED LINE TO DEPTH OF CASING THICKNESS AS SHOWN IN C.   HOLES MARKED 'Z' IN A, TO BE COUNTERSUNK ON THE INNER FACE TO HOLD LEGS OF $\frac{1}{32}$" SPLIT PINS.

up, I vowed in future to lock the worm gear to the driving axle.

I have had a slight urge for a long time to build a LNER 'A3' Pacific. (I've had the drawing for it for 25 years — and the name plates for five years — getting there slowly.) I decided, a few months ago, that I'd like to do something a bit less fiddly than scratch building — for a change. What better than ordering the 'A3' body kit? Remembering the 'King' kit, I decided that I would have another kit from the same manufacturer. Out came the 'A3' drawing, *Locomotives Illustrated*, *Preserved Steam* and one or two other references.

Knowing it would be only a body kit, a mental note was made of where the dividing line between body and chassis would be drawn. The drawers of my spares cabinet were checked out and it was found that one or two 'extras' would be needed, as well as the etched valve gear, worm drive, motor etc. The order was duly sent off.

There would be a wait of several weeks, I started marking out the chassis. Hold it! What pattern of cylinder assembly would be included? Not knowing how much to cut off the frames — that part of the marking out came to a shuddering halt, as I did not want to try cutting cylinder space after the chassis was assembled. There were parts I could work on — the

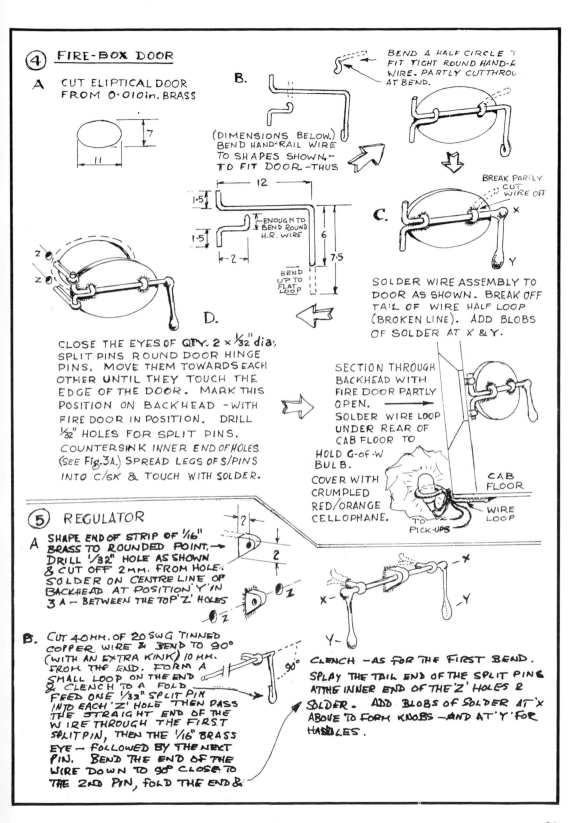

④ **FIRE-BOX DOOR**

A CUT ELIPTICAL DOOR FROM 0·010in. BRASS

7

11

B.

BEND A HALF CIRCLE ? FIT TIGHT ROUND HAND-R WIRE. PARTLY CUT THROU AT BEND.

(DIMENSIONS BELOW.) BEND HAND-RAIL WIRE TO SHAPES SHOWN, — TO FIT DOOR —THUS

12

1·5

1·5

← 2 →

ENOUGH TO BEND ROUND H.R. WIRE

6

7·5

BEND UP TO FLAT LOOP

C.

BREAK PARTLY CUT WIRE OFF

X

Y

SOLDER WIRE ASSEMBLY TO DOOR AS SHOWN. BREAK OFF TAIL OF WIRE HALF LOOP (BROKEN LINE). ADD BLOBS OF SOLDER AT X & Y.

Z

Z

D.

CLOSE THE EYES OF QTY. 2 × 1/32" dia. SPLIT PINS ROUND DOOR HINGE PINS. MOVE THEM TOWARDS EACH OTHER UNTIL THEY TOUCH THE EDGE OF THE DOOR. MARK THIS POSITION ON BACKHEAD — WITH FIRE DOOR IN POSITION. DRILL 1/32" HOLES FOR SPLIT PINS. COUNTERSINK INNER END OF HOLES (SEE Fig.3A.) SPREAD LEGS OF S/PINS INTO C/SK & TOUCH WITH SOLDER.

SECTION THROUGH BACKHEAD WITH FIRE DOOR PARTLY OPEN. SOLDER WIRE LOOP UNDER REAR OF CAB FLOOR TO HOLD G-of-W BULB. COVER WITH CRUMPLED RED/ORANGE CELLOPHANE.

TO PICK-UPS

CAB FLOOR

WIRE LOOP

⑤ **REGULATOR**

2

2

2

A SHAPE END OF STRIP OF 1/16" BRASS TO ROUNDED POINT. DRILL 1/32" HOLE AS SHOWN & CUT OFF 2 MM. FROM HOLE. SOLDER ON CENTRE LINE OF BACKHEAD AT POSITION 'Y' IN 3 A — BETWEEN THE TOP 'Z' HOLES

Z

Z

Z

X

X

Y

Y

B. CUT 40 MM. OF 20 SWG TINNED COPPER WIRE & BEND TO 90° (WITH AN EXTRA KINK) 10 MM. FROM THE END. FORM A SMALL LOOP ON THE END & CLENCH TO A FOLD FEED ONE 1/32" SPLIT PIN INTO EACH 'Z' HOLE THEN PASS THE STRAIGHT END OF THE WIRE THROUGH THE FIRST SPLIT PIN, THEN THE 1/16" BRASS EYE — FOLLOWED BY THE NEXT PIN. BEND THE END OF THE WIRE DOWN TO 90° CLOSE TO THE 2ND PIN, FOLD THE END &

90°

CLENCH — AS FOR THE FIRST BEND. SPLAY THE TAIL END OF THE SPLIT PIN AT THE INNER END OF THE 'Z' HOLES & SOLDER. ADD BLOBS OF SOLDER AT 'X' ABOVE TO FORM KNOBS — AND AT 'Y' FOR HANDLES.

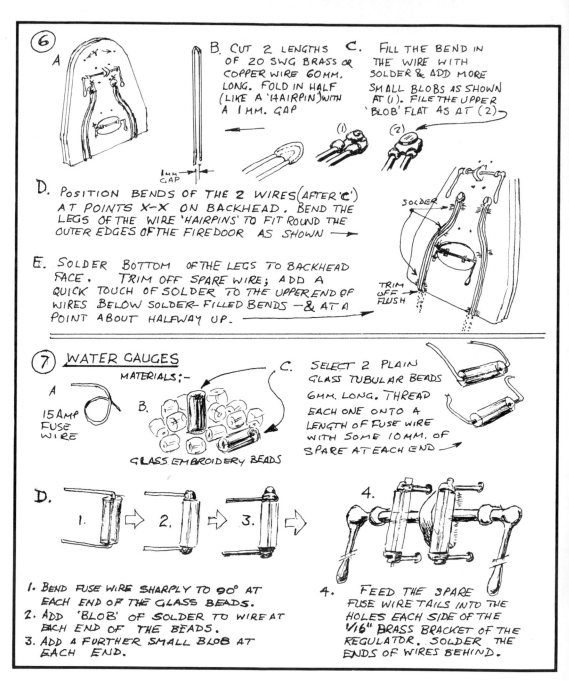

⑥

A.

B. CUT 2 LENGTHS OF 20 SWG BRASS OR COPPER WIRE 60MM. LONG. FOLD IN HALF (LIKE A 'HAIRPIN') WITH A 1MM. GAP

C. FILL THE BEND IN THE WIRE WITH SOLDER & ADD MORE SMALL BLOBS AS SHOWN AT (1). FILE THE UPPER 'BLOB' FLAT AS AT (2)→

1MM GAP

(1) (2)

D. POSITION BENDS OF THE **2** WIRES(AFTER 'C') AT POINTS X-X ON BACKHEAD. BEND THE LEGS OF THE WIRE 'HAIRPINS' TO FIT ROUND THE OUTER EDGES OF THE FIREDOOR AS SHOWN →

SOLDER

E. SOLDER BOTTOM OF THE LEGS TO BACKHEAD FACE. TRIM OFF SPARE WIRE; ADD A QUICK TOUCH OF SOLDER TO THE UPPER END OF WIRES BELOW SOLDER-FILLED BENDS — & AT A POINT ABOUT HALFWAY UP. ————————→

TRIM OFF FLUSH

⑦ WATER GAUGES

MATERIALS:—

A. 15 AMP FUSE WIRE

B.

GLASS EMBROIDERY BEADS

C. SELECT 2 PLAIN GLASS TUBULAR BEADS 6MM. LONG. THREAD EACH ONE ONTO A LENGTH OF FUSE WIRE WITH SOME 10MM. OF SPARE AT EACH END →

D.

1. ⇨ 2. ⇨ 3. ⇨

4.

1. BEND FUSE WIRE SHARPLY TO 90° AT EACH END OF THE GLASS BEADS.
2. ADD 'BLOB' OF SOLDER TO WIRE AT EACH END OF THE BEADS.
3. ADD A FURTHER SMALL BLOB AT EACH END.

4. FEED THE SPARE FUSE WIRE TAILS INTO THE HOLES EACH SIDE OF THE 1/16" BRASS BRACKET OF THE REGULATOR. SOLDER THE ENDS OF WIRES BEHIND.

equaliser frame, motor mount, bogie and pony truck etc.

In the course of time, the kit and 'extras' were received and the parts list was checked. Yes, it was all there as per the list. Then, the parts were compared with the drawing recommended by the manufacturer — which happened to be the same one I'd had for so long. That is where the problems began!

They advised reference to a well known brand of drawing, but for a reason best known to them, decided to make the tender to another drawing. This was the lower sided tender with coal rails. I'd planned for the high sided one. Suffice to say, I would have to scratch-build a new tender body to the original drawing. Rather than be left with just a low sided tender body, I used the underframes as a template and

⑧ STEAM GAUGES:

A.  TIGHTLY ROLL THE END OF SOME 22 SWG COPPER WIRE INTO A SPIRAL UNTIL 3·5MM. DIA: BEND TAIL OF WIRE SHARPLY DOWN TO 90°

3·5

90°

B. FLUX SPIRAL SURFACE & ADD SOLDER TO 'DOME' UP OVER SPIRAL, — THEN, FILE BOTH SIDES FLAT & DRESS OUTER EDGE SQUARE.

C. BEND THE WIRE TAIL BACK & UP TO CENTRE (REAR) OF DIAL, — THEN SHARPLY BACK TO ENTER HOLES 'Y' IN 6A. SOLDER TAILS ONTO INNER FACE OF BACKHEAD & CUT OFF SURPLUS WIRE. CUT WHITE PAPER DISCS (OFFICE PUNCH) & GLUE ONTO SURFACE. INK IN DOTS FOR FIGURES ON DIAL & POINTER. PAINT EDGE & PIPE WITH BRASS PAINT

CUT OFF

C. CLAMP A TIGHT TWIST OF SAME WIRE ROUND PIPE BELOW CONTROL BOX. CUT OFF & SOLDER —

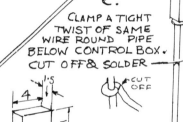

1·5

4

5

CUT OFF

20

⑨ EJECTOR CONTROL (L.H. DRIVE).

A. CUT A SCRAP OF THE 5/32" LEAD SHEET & BEAT OUT TO 1·5MM THICK. CUT RECTANGLE 5MM. X 4MM. X 1·5MM.

B.1. DRILL 1/32" HOLE UP IN BOTTOM EDGE — 1 MM. IN FROM L.H. SIDE & 2 MM. DEEP.

B.2. SOLDER 20MM OF 22 SWG TINNED COPPER WIRE IN HOLE

D. ADD 2 BLOBS OF SOLDER TO TOP EDGE & ONE TO FACE — JUST ABOVE LEFT OF CENTRE.

E. LAY END OF 26 SWG WIRE ON FACE BLOB & TOUCH QUICKLY WITH HOT IRON — TO SOLDER WIRE WITHOUT SPREADING THE FACE BLOB.

CUT OFF

F. SOLDER END OF 26 SWG WIRE TO TOP RH BLOB, AS DONE IN **E.** BEND END OF WIRE TO DISAPPEAR BEHIND L.H. STEAM GAUGE. FLATTEN TOP OF OTHER BLOB.

G. DRILL 1/16" HOLE X 1MM DEEP IN FORWARD FACE OF CONTROL — AS NEAR OUTER EDGE AS POSSIBLE & HALFWAY UP. THE EJECTOR PIPE FITS HERE.

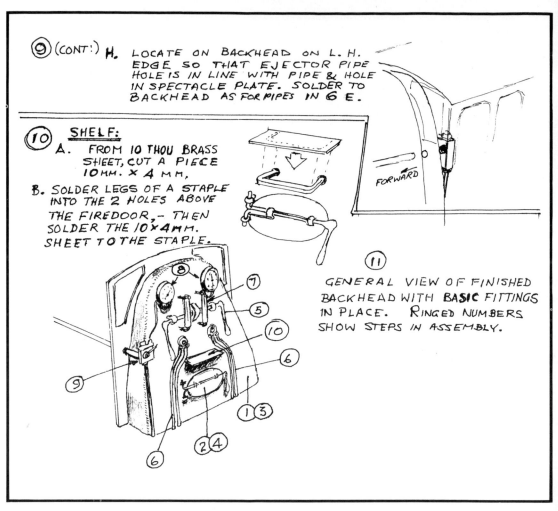

(9) (CONT.) **H.** LOCATE ON BACKHEAD ON L.H. EDGE SO THAT EJECTOR PIPE HOLE IS IN LINE WITH PIPE & HOLE IN SPECTACLE PLATE. SOLDER TO BACKHEAD AS FOR PIPES IN 6 E.

(10) **SHELF:**
A. FROM 10 THOU BRASS SHEET, CUT A PIECE 10 MM. × 4 MM.

B. SOLDER LEGS OF A STAPLE INTO THE 2 HOLES ABOVE THE FIREDOOR, — THEN SOLDER THE 10×4MM. SHEET TO THE STAPLE.

FORWARD

(11) GENERAL VIEW OF FINISHED BACKHEAD WITH **BASIC** FITTINGS IN PLACE. RINGED NUMBERS SHOW STEPS IN ASSEMBLY.

built a complete tender — leaving a full tender kit (minus axle guards) to go into stock, in case some day I decided to build an 'A1'.

The next item to come to hand was the cast smokebox door. Aha! I thought. That's the front end, now, where is the backhead for the cab end of things? Surely, the backhead is as important a part of a body kit as the smokebox door? So, I then checked the parts list again, but it was not listed. Not listed, then it was not officially 'missing'. Next check was the firebox casing. The makers had again departed from the drawing. By finishing the firebox casing at the front wall of the cab. The prototype firebox extends into the cab and, in designing my chassis, I had already used that area for motor clearance. Their cab front wall was a full width panel to which the firebox casing could be soldered leaving a blank front wall inside the cab, as well as being 7mm shorter than I needed for clearance.

There was only one thing to do. From the drawing dimensions, I marked out the outline of the firebox casing on the front cab wall. (There is not much of the spectacle plate outside the firebox.) Now, I had also to make a new firebox casing — long enough to extend into the cab — from 10thou brass sheet. (You get a very funny look here in New Zealand if you ask the metal supplier if there is any nickel-silver sheet about. More on these suppliers later.) I made the casing, cut away the cab front and was agreeably surprised to find that it fitted at first go. In addition to this part, I was not happy with the over-large motor gap under the tapered section of the boiler — and the way it fitted to the firebox casing — which had been given extra flaps to bend in towards the boiler. Thus, it did not match mine. So, a new tapered section of boiler had to be made.

Now, I turned to the section supplied for the smokebox/parallel front end of the boiler, then found that, according to the recommended drawing, plus three others, the supplied part was too small in diameter. The large brass washer supplied as the smokebox front was, according to the drawings, the right diameter. When the kit boiler was wrapped round it, (to give the right boiler diameter) there was an ⅛in gap along the bottom seam. So, once more into the breach . . . to make a parallel section. Now, all the boiler from the smokebox front to the backhead in the cab was scratch-built.

At this stage of pondering the next move, I idly 'doodled' a sketch of what I had used of the body kit. Fig 1A is the result. What was left of the sheet metal parts of the kit, I could easily have fabricated myself, as I had done so many times before. I had the idea, originally, to build a kit as a change from a lot of 'fiddly' work, but finished up doing this nonetheless.

I turned to the cylinder assembly, hoping for some relief. Here the two halves of the cylinders in no way matched. In addition, the outside shape would have been more suited to a Stanier or Fowler pattern than one of the Gresley type. So, back to the drawing board to draw up the parts needed to fabricate a cylinder assembly, 25 parts, counting the new (smaller) crossheads and more robust piston rods than the fragile things included in the kit. (See Fig 1B.)

I did get two whistles in the kit, but no safety valves — which had to be turned up on my trusty old Myford ML3 lathe of over 40 years service. I also have to make my own 8BA and smaller screws and nuts as, the local supplier has never heard of that size. (2, 4 and 6BA) are 'discovered' from some obscure recess behind the counter if pressed for them.) Anyway, by making my own screws, I get the length I want as well as the head shape/size — rather than having to modify standard cheese-head screws.

Well, having extended the firebox into the cab, I now needed a backhead. So, that was made as a separate project. There follows, for those other modellers who find themselves with a large empty cab or a firebox with no back in it, a series of diagrams showing all the steps in making a backhead for an 'A3'. Of course, not everyone with an empty firebox will be in the process of making an 'A3' model, but the same system can be followed — with the aid of a photograph or diagram of the type being made. The dimensions given here are for an 'A3' and may not be the same for other types.

This backhead was made from an old fishing weight — which, in turn, had been made from ⁵⁄₃₂in sheet lead. It is meant to be representative only, not fully detailed, but enough to pass as the right thing to the average viewer. 'Rivet counters' are not invited. I will not dwell on the painting — this will be to the individual modeller's own ideas.

A nice finish to round off with, is a grain of wheat bulb mounted inside the firebox and covered with orange/red cellophane. It is wired across the pick-up wires, so that, when running and the firebox door is open, a nice red glow can be seen. It gives a realistic glow on the tracks below also, though this can be masked off if not wanted.

Finally, the question. Can this be called a kit-built model? So much for my desire to make, for once, something less 'fiddly' than scratch. But, if some other modellers have gained something from my frustrations, all is not lost. Perhaps I should go over to RTR?

Heathfield

The Heathfield exhibition layout of the Chatham & District Model Railway Club appeared at several shows in the South East including the 1971 National Model Railway Exhibition.

The prototype station served the largest of the towns on the line between Tunbridge Wells and Eastbourne. The route lies on the border of the former SER and LBSCR territories. When the Tunbridge Wells & Eastbourne Railway Co was promoting the line it was hoped that the LBSCR would lease it and provide the rolling stock. The latter Company was not interested, however, as they already possessed a satisfactory route to Eastbourne. It was only when the SER came into the picture and threatened to capture part of the Eastbourne traffic that the Brighton Company took over the line. The pattern of traffic remained unchanged for many years until electrification of the main line by the Southern Railway in 1933. British Railways closed part of the line and Heathfield was used as the terminus for goods traffic only until complete closure in 1965.

Eighteen stations of a similar style were built during the 1880s, five of which were on this line. In their original condition the upper stories were finished in a Tudor half-timbered style but in the early part of this century, were covered over with decorative hanging tiles.

Construction of the layout mainly follows usual practices; however, for exhibition work we prefer a solid base of soft wood framing covered with ½in chipboard and ½in medium hardboard. This is sold under the trade name of Sundeala, and we find it takes fixing pins better than insulation board. Trackwork is of soldered construction using copper-coated paxolin sleepers and is ballasted with a thick mixture of granulated cork and wallpaper paste. In order to capture accurately the atmosphere of the prototype, all the buildings are hand-made, mainly from card. The roof and wall tiling, typical of the architecture of this line, was formed by applying card strips to the model, the strips previously being cut either with a modelling knife to produce square tiles or by

Below:
Heathfield signalbox with 'B4' 0-4-0T No 102.

making a double cut with a pair of pinking shears to form the patterned tiles. This work took some 250 hours to complete.

Signalling of the layout is by Southern Railway pattern rail-built signals, constructed by a club member, using Tri-ang relays to operate the arms.

Heathfield, built as part of a larger continuous layout developed over a period of years from a single track branch also formed a layout on its own as a terminus, thus representing the prototypically shortened

Above:
An exterior view of Heathfield station building.

Below:
A view of Heathfield station in June 1965 — the year of its complete closure. *John Scrace*

branch of later years. Whilst performing satisfactorily, operation has been somewhat restricted in the continuous layout form, by the single track running.

Michael Varley

Anatomy of a Photo

There are railway enthusiasts who insist that Sir Nigel Gresley's 'A4' locomotive was superior even to the LMS 'Duchesses', and it was with them in mind that I determined to make a picture of one. I wanted to capture some of the wonder and atmosphere of an 'A4' speeding past our vantage point by the trackside.

The locomotive is the old Hornby-Dublo three-rail version, in Garter blue livery and bearing the name of its designer. I bought it from a former schoolfriend in 1958 and after getting it home I discovered too late that it needed remagnetising, but have never got round to it. The first two coaches were picked up recently at a car boot sale. Both locomotive and coaches date from the immediate postwar period and the only sign of age other than fair wear and tear is the moulded plastic top to the tender which has warped a little. The third coach is a later one in British Railways carmine and cream livery, but its shape was going to be more obvious than its colour.

SMP OO track was laid on the fibreboard base and the train marshalled on it. The board was supported in the middle and allowed to sag at each end to give the impression of a train reaching the summit of a long gradient. Discarded clothing was placed to left and right to suggest rising ground and to provide a visual stop, and plain white paper was supported behind to make a clear sky. When the lights were turned on, it was very obvious that the tinplate coaches were reflecting the white

Below:
The finished photograph proves extremely effective even without the benefit of modern 'scale' stock. *Author*

Far right:
For comparison, a view of the whole negative before cropping. *Author*

backdrop where they shouldn't, so some black trousers were used to obstruct this where they could not be seen. (On reading this over it sounds like instructions for nude photography, but I do assure you that this is not the case!)

The lighting was a No 1 photoflood (275W) in a metal reflector about 4ft from the model. Another reflector carried a 100W bulb for fill-in, ie to soften hard shadows, and was placed near the camera.

Now, how to suggest movement? A number of ideas put themselves forward and were promptly rejected as being totally impractical — they will be tried in due course. This time it would have to be simple. The First Aid cupboard was raided for cotton wool which was teased out and the pointed end pushed into the locomotive chimney. Of course it flopped everywhere except where it was wanted. So the next attempt was to thread it on a short piece of wire to support it. Further small pieces were placed, and re-placed, on the carriage roofs so that the smoke looked continuous.

The Pentax was loaded with Ilford FP4 film (rated at ISO 50) and screwed to the tripod. It was adjusted for height until eye level was somewhere near the top of the coupled wheels. From now on it was a matter of fiddling around until things looked right. A piece of fencing and a telegraph pole were tried beyond the locomotive, and the telegraph pole was later discarded. The main light was moved around so that the wheels could be seen and its final position was above and to the left of the camera. To be sure that I was not missing anything, I tried every lens I have and settled on the 28mm wide angle set at f22. Focus was sharpest on the valve gear and the cable release fired the shutter. The camera decided on about half a second exposure, and I was happy to go along with it as it is so much better than I am at working out such things.

Development was for seven and a half minutes in Aculux and the negative was enlarged on to Multigrade paper with the grade three filter in place. It became very obvious at this stage that the track ended about six scale feet in front of the engine, so I had to be more selective than I had expected for the final picture. The telegraph pole made the picture appear too static for the feeling of movement which I had planned, so the picture appears without it.

There are few pictures which do not benefit from the judicious use of a pair of scissors or a guillotine, and the same holds true if you do your own enlarging. The picture should be harmonious, it should tell a simple story without any conflicting elements, and the composition should be pleasing. Very often this can be improved by removing a strip from one or both sides, or from the top or bottom. You would want to practice first by covering up the bit you are thinking of removing with a piece of card before taking the irrevocable step with the scissors! You may find two 'L' shaped pieces of card useful, placed face to face to make an adjustable rectangle, through which you can view the picture. When you are satisfied with the result, a straight edge and a craft knife will perform the operation, and you then have a little gem of a picture instead of an assorted collection of images.

The tone of the 'sky' can be controlled when the picture is taken, by allowing more or less light to fall on the white background paper. If you keep it in darkness it will appear almost black and this can be very dramatic. In this case, the corners of the sky were darkened a little bit under the enlarger by covering up the centre of the picture and letting the light from the negative fall on the corners for about twice as long, just to emphasise the steam effect and to keep the interest well within the picture.

Finally, dust marks, hairs, blemishes and unwanted highlights were painted out with black water colour and a fine brush, matching the colour with the gum from an envelope.

I won't pretend the picture is perfect, but I think I have achieved what I set out to do. The lack of distracting clutter in both background and foreground concentrates our attention on the subject, while the smoke, the perspective and the viewpoint suggest speed, power and size.

I have quite deliberately used the model in 'straight from the box' condition (even if it has taken a quarter of a century) to show that atmosphere can be created without a lot of hard work on details such as lamps and that coupling link. These can easily be fixed, but it is the coarse scale wheels which really give it all away.

If there is any case for P4 standards, this is surely it.

John Broadley

Novel Method of wiring a Reverse Loop

By way of adding a further novelty to the electrical side of reverse loops, I would like to offer a method of dealing with these which has been passed by Colworth electronics for use with their automatic shuttle module. This is normally used for working a single-line branch automatically and has a parallel switching facility which allows colour light signals to change in phase with the shuttle sequence. The module employed is the ACM-3S type without 'soft start' facility and it is connected to the reverse loop portion of the layout at the 'neck' in place of the usual double-pole double-throw (DPDT) switch with crossed connections.

In order to be aware of the alignment of polarity whether set for incoming or outgoing traffic — two colour light signals (two-aspect) are situated, one at the 'starter' position and one guarding re-entry to the neck — I used old Hornby-Dublo signals. Spare bulbs are obtainable as Marklin spares and I substituted an amber for the green bulb in a 'home' signal as is correct for a terminus approach and completed the effect using an illuminated buffer stop, again old Hornby-Dublo (ex-swapmeet).

The result is interesting because an adjustable time delay is provided. An incoming train is halted at the red signal until it changes to amber. An outgoing train departs on the green aspect. I discovered that if a switch is incorporated into the 'clock' circuit of the module (the power supply) you always get the same aspect displayed immediately after switching 'off' which is good for preventing accidental polarity reversal before a train has come to rest.

Incidentally, it does not matter whether conventional or Zero 1 control is applied to the C terminals of the module but only 12V dc or 16V ac should be applied to the power input which has separate pairs of tags for either.

Obviously this approach to an old problem can be applied to a triangle to allow 'hands off' switching of points and polarity but watch the power consumption of the point solenoids (which should be wired 'end/off' like the Fleischmann Profi range) and use a relay if necessary.

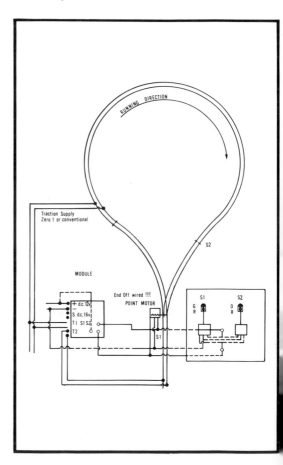

W. J. Wilson

LNER Bogie Sides in 2mm Scale

Continuing the saga of the LNER coach sides photographed down to 2mm scale (*Model Railway Constructor*, July 1984) a further idea, born of desperation, has come to light.

Having constructed the coaches and placed them on my stock of LNER bogies, in no way did they perform satisfactorily. The three-car articulated buffet car set kept falling over on a particular curve and odd coaches kept coming off the track at various points. This was despite the fact that I had changed the plastic wheels for the Grafar all-metal type.

Now, ready-made LNER bogies are unobtainable in 2mm scale or N gauge, so, what to do

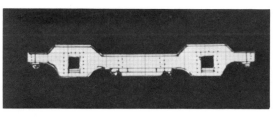

Above:
The bogie sideframe drawn out on graph paper as a template.

Below:
Multiple sideframe drawings on grey paper (left) and black paper (right).

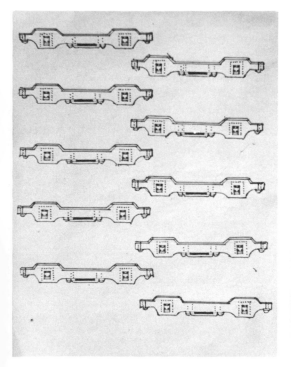

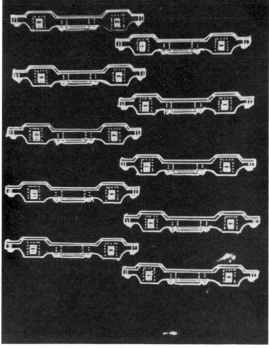

next? Remembering my experience with the coach sides, I wondered if it would be possible to do the same with the bogie sides. Grafar had recently produced a very good N gauge coach bogie with metal wheels and sprung couplings. So, I obtained a set of these and tried them out on an LNER coaching set with excellent results. At the same time I cut out a 2mm LNER bogie shape and stuck it to one of the bogie sides and it looked quite acceptable, so I decided to explore the possibility of photographing the sides in 2mm scale.

A 10-coach LNER train has 20 bogies, and each bogie has two sides, so at least 40 sides need to be produced for one train. Multiply my trains by at least six, plus any more productions, and you will see that a large number of sides need to be made. Bearing this in mind, I reckoned I would need a template to start with, so on a squared sheet of paper, with a 4mm carriage drawing handy, I copied out the bogie side to 8mm scale. That is twice the length and breadth of the drawing. This gave me plenty of room for putting in the details, such as axleboxes, rivet heads, etc. Having perfected this, I then cut it out about 10mm from the drawing all the way round. Obtaining a 10thou sheet of Plastikard and a bottle of Mekpak, I welded on the drawing and waited until the Mekpak was dry. I then cut out the axle boxes, leaving two square holes. This was done so that I could mark in the axle boxes exactly in place in each copy to be photographed. Next I cut round the edge of the bogie side exactly.

If you are making a 'Silver Jubilee' set you will doubtless know that the bogie sides were grey in colour. So I obtained a sheet of grey paper about 240mm by 30mm and also one of black paper of the same size. Take the template and draw round on the paper the exact shape of at least 10 outlines, not forgetting to draw in the axleboxes. Next put in all the details on each outline. On the grey sheet I used a black felt tip and on the black sheet I used silver, which showed up particularly well. You may of course do more drawings on a larger size of paper as you can certainly get more in on the camera viewfinder.

Next you have to calculate how to photograph them so that they will appear the correct size. The prints are 150mm by 100mm, and the bogie sides are 28mm long, which is approximately a quarter. So if you multiply the length of your drawing by four you obtain a distance of approximately 460mm. (Drawing round the template has increased the size a little.) This is the width which must appear in your viewfinder. If you place a ruler so that 460mm lies across, and just appears in the viewfinder, you will be about correct. All you have to do now is to photograph the number of bogie sides you require on colour film and wait for the arrival of the prints.

Now comes the tedious part of cutting them to shape and glueing them in position. I found that a cutting knife is quicker than scissors and Bostik Clear adhesive is best for fixing them in place. Purists can, of course, build up the axleboxes and any other details, but as the sides are so small the drawn details give quite a good impression. The white axleboxes and rivet heads might appear to be very pronounced, but if you look at photographs of LNER coaches you will see that the bogie shapes are emphasised by the sunshine and shadow. The exaggeration is not too excessive. When you come to sticking them on you will notice a discrepancy with the axleboxes. The ones on the Grafar bogies are wider apart than the LNER type, but with your coach in position and the wheels on the track, it is difficult to notice.

Working along this theme of using photographs, I am experimenting with tender sides, putting in the lettering, and then doing the lining with a pen and ruler. Also I have been considering locomotives as well. The boiler and bands can be wrapped round a metal tube and the cab sides can be photographed with the number in position. Perhaps other experimenters can get in touch with me, through letters to the Editor, if they have achieved anything worthwhile. The possibilities are enormous.

Below:
Completed bogies mounted on the frames.

Peter Kazmierczak

Forgotten Diesel-hydraulics

Ask anyone to name three types of diesel-hydraulic locomotive and most people would answer 'Western', 'Warship' and 'Hymek'. Whilst it was the larger express types which grabbed the limelight, there were also some other less well known locomotives which employed hydraulic transmission.

Although the Western Region was not the only region to employ hydraulic transmission: for example the St Pancras-Bedford DMUs and some small 0-4-0 shunters based on the Scottish and London Midland Regions used this type of transmission, it was the only one to use this type of drive for its main line diesel fleet. Individual as ever, with the 1955 Modernisation Plan the WR ordered 14 diesel-hydraulic locomotives to test the merits of this form of traction in Britain. These 14 were in three classes:

  North British-built 2,000hp A1A-A1A
    Nos D600-D604
  Swindon-built 2,000hp B-B Nos D800-802
  North British-built 1,000hp B-B
    Nos D6300-6305
With the increasing pace of modernisation, even before some of these engines appeared in

Below:
NBL Type 2 diesel-hydraulics Nos D6316 and D6319 in original green livery at Penzance shed. The folding disc headcode indicators are clearly visible. Note also the diamond-shaped North British worksplates. *C. J. Blay*

service, further orders were placed for these and other types. This led to the large and varied hydraulic fleet, the last members of which lingered on until withdrawal in February 1977.

The first class which I want to look at is one of the original hydraulic designs, the North British 1,000hp B-B which later became (and are better known as) Class 22.

Class 22

Although not the most handsome of diesel designs, the class was a familiar sight in the West Country on all manner of trains for over a decade. For a time they were also an everyday sight in the hallowed precincts of Paddington itself. A total of 58 were built by the North British Locomotive Co in Glasgow, entering service between January 1959 and November 1962. The first six (Nos D6300-05) were of 1,000hp whilst the main production batch (Nos D6306-57) were uprated to 1,100hp.

Allocation and work

With the exception of No D6300 which was initially allocated to Swindon, this class has only ever been allocated to four depots. The following illustrates the distribution of the Class 22s at five different dates:

Below:
No D6301, the second member of the class was the first to be withdrawn, in December 1967. It is seen in store at Laira depot on 11 June 1967. Small yellow warning panels have been applied, but the original disc indicators remain. The first six members of the class differed in many visible respects from the later examples, eg body side grilles, windscreen wipers and various front end details.
D. Percival

Above right:
Another of the first six, No D6302, fitted with four-character headcode boxes, in green livery with large yellow warning panels. The warning panels extend to the headcode boxes, which are positioned higher than on the main batch from No D6306 onwards.

Below right:
During the period of dieselisation in the West Country, steam and diesel combinations were quite common. D6336 in standard green livery with yellow warning panels pilots 2-6-2T No 6148 on the 08.10 Taunton-Minehead at Bishops Lydeard on 22 August 1964.
M. J. Fox

31/12/59 (7)	31/12/62 (58)	31/12/65 (58)	31/12/68 (30)	31/12/71 (4)
Laira = 100%	Laira = 64% Newton Abbot = 21% Bath Road = 15%	Laira = 40% Newton Abbot = 24% Old Oak Common = 36%	Laira = 33% Newton Abbot = 20% Bath Road = 7% Old Oak Common = 40%	Laira = 100%

Initially the class was concentrated on Laira depot in Plymouth and this was always one of their strongholds. In 1959 and 1960 they rarely strayed from Devon and Cornwall. Some of their first duties involved banking and piloting work over the infamous Dainton and Hemerdon banks between Newton Abbot and Plymouth. At this time it was a common sight to see one of these diesels piloting a 'King' or a 'Castle' over these South Devon banks. Beauty and the beast one might say, although I'll leave it up to you to decide which was which. Meanwhile in Cornwall they sometimes appeared on the main line working in multiple on some of the expresses. However, their more usual duties were working local passenger and freight trains on the Cornish branches. St Ives, Newquay, Falmouth, and in particular Helston, all saw members of the class.

Newton Abbot received its first allocation in January 1961 and Bath Road shed in Bristol got some in 1962. Gradually the class appeared on

An interim livery variation was BR blue with yellow warning panels and a small BR double arrow. No D6327 heads a weed-killing train through Newbury station on 28 April 1967. *D. E. Canning*

more lines in the West Country. With the demise of steam from the ex-LSWR lines in North Devon and Cornwall it was the NBL Type 2 which took over many of the workings, be it ballast from Meldon, holidaymakers to Ilfracombe or freight to Wadebridge. In the Bristol area they could be seen ambling to Avonmouth, pottering along to Portishead, wandering down to Wells or just mooching around Malago Vale.

September 1963 saw their sphere of influence increase as they began to be allocated to Old Oak Common shed in London. By the end of the following year most of the empty coaching stock workings in and out of Paddington were in their hands. As can be seen in the allocation diagram, by the end of 1965 Bristol had lost all its NBL Type 2s. However, in 1966 they began to filter back, but this time to some new haunts, especially in the Gloucester area.

Withdrawals began in December 1967 with D6301 which had been at Laira all its life. By the end of 1968 only 30 were left. Most of these went in 1971 leaving only four at Laira to see in 1972. However, they didn't see much of the New Year as they were all officially withdrawn on 1 January. All were subsequently cut up for scrap, none being preserved.

Variations

The body sides of the original batch, D6300-D6305, differed quite noticeably from the remainder of the class due to internal variations. The cab fronts also display differences and the main areas are outlined in one of the diagrams.

D6300-05:
  i) Windscreen wipers pivot from the bottom edge of the screen.
  ii) Headcode discs originally fitted but most subsequently fitted with twin headcode boxes.
  iii) Vents on cab nose set in line with central lamp bracket.

D6306-33:
  i) Windscreen wipers pivot from the top of the screen.
  i) Originally fitted with headcode discs but later all altered by the addition of headcode boxes. This caused the top handrails to be relocated.
  iii) Vents on cab nose set in line with bottom lamp brackets.

D6334-57: Fitted with headcode boxes when built.

Livery Details

Again the main differences are shown on one of the diagrams but perhaps I can add a few notes to amplify my sketches.

All the class were turned out in green livery. On the first six, because of the bodyside louvres, the British Railways crest was applied in the only position available — by the side of one of the cab doors. The rest of the class had the crest in a more orthodox position nearer the centre of

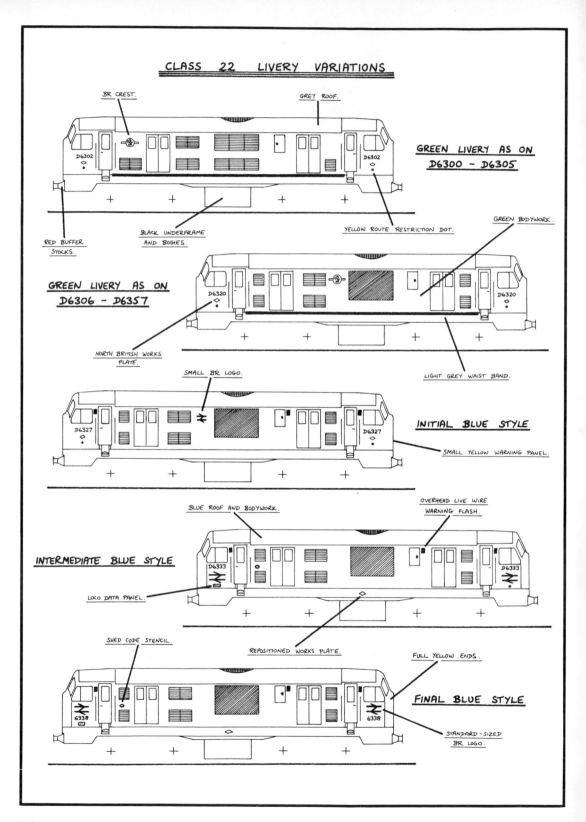

CLASS 22 LIVERY VARIATIONS

BR CREST.

GREY ROOF.

D6302 · D6302

GREEN LIVERY AS ON D6300 — D6305

RED BUFFER STOCKS.

BLACK UNDERFRAME AND BOGIES.

YELLOW ROUTE RESTRICTION DOT.

GREEN BODYWORK.

GREEN LIVERY AS ON D6306 — D6357

D6320 · D6320

NORTH BRITISH WORKS PLATE.

LIGHT GREY WAIST BAND.

SMALL BR LOGO.

D6327 · D6327

INITIAL BLUE STYLE

SMALL YELLOW WARNING PANEL.

BLUE ROOF AND BODYWORK.

OVERHEAD LIVE WIRE WARNING FLASH.

INTERMEDIATE BLUE STYLE

D6333 · D6333

LOCO DATA PANEL.

REPOSITIONED WORKS PLATE.

SHED CODE STENCIL.

FULL YELLOW ENDS.

6338 · 6338

FINAL BLUE STYLE

STANDARD-SIZED BR LOGO.

Above:
No D6326 in blue livery with four-character headcode arrangement nears the end of its working life shunting Cholsey & Moulsford yard on 23 June 1970. *J. H. Bird*

the body. During 1962 small yellow warning panels began to be applied to the cab nose. As construction of the class was still proceeding in that year it follows that some had this yellow panel from new. Also in 1962 the overhead live wire flashes began to appear on the class — three on each side and two on the front.

1966 saw the first examples being turned out of Swindon Works in the then new blue livery. However, only a small BR logo was applied to the bodyside and these initial repaints retained their small yellow warning panels. Sample numbers in this style included D6314 and D6327. Soon Swindon was giving the class the now familiar full yellow ends. Also larger BR logos were applied to each of the cab sides and this entailed the removal of the four diamond-shaped North British worksplates. Two of these were repositioned centrally on the body above the fuel tank. Sample numbers in this 'intermediate' style include D6328, D6334, D6339, D6343 and D6354. The final blue style appeared in about 1970 with the locomotive number (without the 'D' prefix) beneath the BR logo. Sample numbers in this type included 6326, 6330, 6338, 6352 and 6356.

About half of the Class 22s were repainted in one blue style or another. Hence on withdrawal many of the class were still in green with small yellow warning panels. However, a couple were given full yellow ends whilst still retaining green; an example being D6331.

Modelling the Class 22

The only model I know of this class is the MTK cast metal kit in 4mm scale. No ready-to-run models are presently available. However in N gauge Langley Miniature Models have a kit of the Class 29 whilst Hornby have a ready-to-run version of the Class 29 in OO gauge. With a lot of work it is possible to convert the Class 29 into a Class 22. A most detailed and comprehensive article on this appeared in the June/July 1981 issues of *Model Railway Constructor* — for anyone attempting the conversion I strongly advise you to read that article first.

An even more forgotten diesel-hydraulic design is the Class 14. An interesting feature of both these classes is that they were the last new locomotives to be built at their respective works. Class 22 No D6357 was the last locomotive built by the North British Co at Glasgow whilst D9555 (the last Class 14) was the final locomotive built at Swindon for BR. A rather sad end to two great locomotive works.

CLASS 22   CAB FRONT VARIATIONS

AS ON D6300 – D6305

AS ON D6306 – D6333

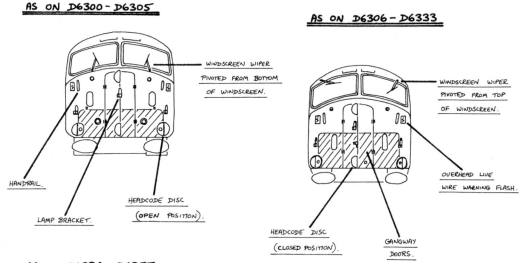

WINDSCREEN WIPER PIVOTED FROM BOTTOM OF WINDSCREEN.

HANDRAIL.

LAMP BRACKET.

HEADCODE DISC (OPEN POSITION).

WINDSCREEN WIPER PIVOTED FROM TOP OF WINDSCREEN.

OVERHEAD LIVE WIRE WARNING FLASH.

HEADCODE DISC (CLOSED POSITION).

GANGWAY DOORS.

AS ON D6334 – D6357

LATER MODIFICATIONS TO D6306 – D6333

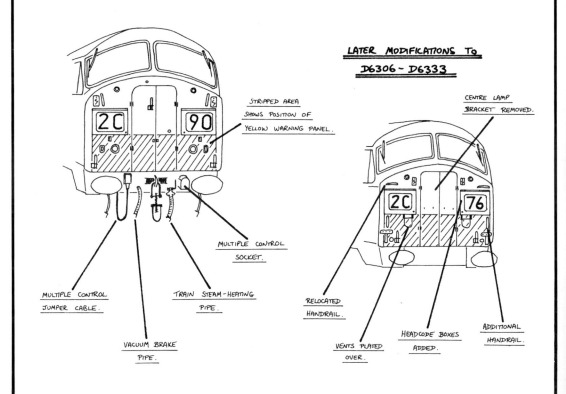

STRIPPED AREA SHOWS POSITION OF YELLOW WARNING PANEL.

MULTIPLE CONTROL SOCKET.

MULTIPLE CONTROL JUMPER CABLE.

TRAIN STEAM-HEATING PIPE.

VACUUM BRAKE PIPE.

CENTRE LAMP BRACKET REMOVED.

RELOCATED HANDRAIL.

VENTS PLATED OVER.

HEADCODE BOXES ADDED.

ADDITIONAL HANDRAIL.

Above:
Ex-works in the final standard livery applied to Class 22, No 6352 stands at Gloucester Horton Road depot on 19 March 1970. Double arrow symbols are positioned below the cab side windows. The D prefix has been
dropped and numbers are in the 1967 British Rail alphabet (compare with previous illustrations). Below the locomotive number on the left-hand end is the data panel transfer. Bogies, buffers and cab-door kick plates are painted black. *N. E. Preedy*

Class 14

By the time this class had entered traffic, the work for which it had been originally designed had virtually disappeared. Hence their life in BR ownership was very short, being less than five years from when the first one appeared, to when the last one was withdrawn. In the Type 1 power bracket with a rating of 650hp, 56 of these locomotives, numbered between D9500 and D9555 were built at Swindon in 1964/65.

Allocation and Work
Apart from one allocated to Severn Tunnel Junction for a while, the class was only allocated to five depots. The distribution at various dates is:

31/12/64 (25)	31/12/66 (56)	31/12/68 (11)
Canton = 64% Bath Road = 20% Old Oak Common = 16%	Canton = 37% Bath Road = 18% Landore = 9% Dairycoates = 36%	Canton = 55% Landore = 45%

At first the class was divided between Old Oak Common, Bath Road and Canton shed in Cardiff. Without any form of train heating and

with a maximum speed of 40mph, the Class 14s were designed for trip working, local freight and shunting duties. Those based at Old Oak Common tended to work on local freights in the Reading and Didcot areas whilst those at Bristol often appeared on workings from Gloucester to Stroud and Nailsworth, and also to the Forest of Dean.

Those based in South Wales, initially at Canton and from 1965 also at Landore depot in Swansea, operated many trip workings between coal mines in the Welsh Valleys. However, with both railway lines and collieries closing the Western Region soon had a surplus of this type of locomotive. Hence, in December 1966, there was a block transfer of over 33% of the class to Dairycoates shed in Hull.

However, the North Eastern Region did not really know what to do with them either, and most were withdrawn in April 1968. A few lasted another year in South Wales before final withdrawal in April 1969. Fortunately less than 10 were actually cut up for scrap, the majority were sold either to the National Coal Board or the British Steel Corporation for further industrial use. Since then several have been preserved for use on private lines.

Variations

As they had such a short life on BR there were not any real variations within the class. Excluding one-offs, I wonder if this is the only diesel class without differences between individual members?

Livery Details

Here again no real variations. Originally they were turned out with a light green cab, the bonnets on either side being standard green.

Black and yellow chevrons were painted on the bonnet ends. The bufferbeam was red and the underframe black. The circular British Railways coaching stock symbol was applied to the cabside with the number below, and overhead

live wire flashes were fitted from new. The drawing shows the position of these features. Finally the handrails and steps were picked out in white.

None were repainted in rail blue. I have never seen any photographs of these locomotives in BR service in anything other than their original green livery.

Modelling the Class 14

Not surprisingly, as far as I can tell no

Above:
Class 14 No D9530 at Newport on 10 July 1968. This locomotive was withdrawn in October of the same year, having only entered service in February 1965.
N. E. Preedy

ready-to-run models or kits of this prototype are available in any scale. Indeed I have never seen a scratchbuilt model of this class. Has anyone ever made a Class 14? With its angular bonnets it shouldn't be too difficult to fabricate out of

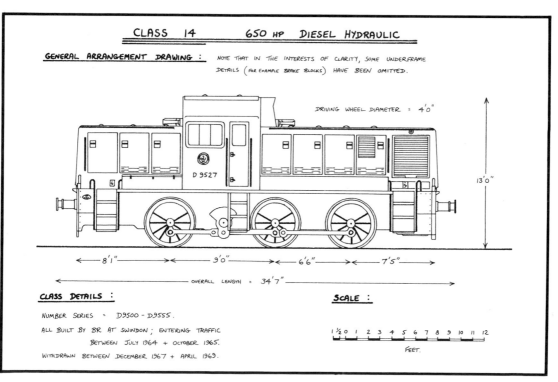

CLASS 14   650 HP DIESEL HYDRAULIC

GENERAL ARRANGEMENT DRAWING : NOTE THAT IN THE INTERESTS OF CLARITY, SOME UNDERFRAME DETAILS (FOR EXAMPLE BRAKE BLOCKS) HAVE BEEN OMITTED.

DRIVING WHEEL DIAMETER = 4'0"

D 9527

13'0"

← 8'1" → ← 9'0" → ← 6'6" → ← 7'5" →

OVERALL LENGTH = 34'7"

CLASS DETAILS :

NUMBER SERIES = D9500 - D9555.

ALL BUILT BY BR AT SWINDON ; ENTERING TRAFFIC BETWEEN JULY 1964 + OCTOBER 1965.

WITHDRAWN BETWEEN DECEMBER 1967 + APRIL 1969.

SCALE :

1½ 0 1 2 3 4 5 6 7 8 9 10 11 12

FEET.

metal or plastikard. It might even be possible (in 4mm scale) to use the old Tri-ang 0-6-0 chassis as a basis although the jackshaft drive might be a little difficult to reproduce. However it could be omitted as it's partly hidden by the steps leading up into the cab.

I hope that I've awakened some memories of these two diesel-hydraulic classes. Gone but perhaps not forgotten.

Finally if any manufacturers are reading this, how about a ready-to-run model in 4mm scale of one of these classes — in particular the Class 22? It would make a change from all those duplicated 'Westerns' and 'Warships'.

Below:
An unidentified member of the class in NCB service at Ashington colliery in 1971. A number of the examples which were sold into industrial service have since gone on to new lives on preserved railways. *M. Dunnett*

The Midland Railway in the Wye Valley

A delve in the unlisted Real Photographs negatives recently revealed several views of the former Midland Railway line from Hereford to Three Cocks Junction. By the time these photographs were taken the route had become part of the Western Region, yet apart from chocolate and cream paint, the pure Midland character survived, and presents interesting and so far as we are aware, untapped inspiration for a layout. These unlisted views are supplemented here by a number of other photographs of the line.

Above:
This 1933 view of Hay-on-Wye from the footbridge shows a well kept and moderately busy country station, in stark contrast with the following photograph. One of several noteworthy features is the nameboard, which reads: HAY CHANGE FOR THE GOLDEN VALLEY LINE. The Golden Valley Railway ran to Pontrilas on the GWR Newport-Hereford line and closed to passenger services in December 1941. *L&GRP (11859)*

Below:
Despite the Western Region colours, the timber station building, water tank, lamps and nameboards retain their distinctly non-GWR origins in this bleak view looking west in May 1963. *Ian Allan Library*

Above:
A rather different style of timber building was used for the station at Whitney-on-the-Wye, seen here in 1932.
L&GRP (13770)

Below:
Whitney station again in May 1963, after neglect and dereliction had begun to set in.
Ian Allan Library

Left:
A fine and apparently well kept yard crane stands amid the undergrowth at Whitney-on-the Wye.
Ian Allan Library

Below:
The steel bridge over the River Wye at Whitney.
Ian Allan Library

Bottom:
A charming view of the attractive and well-tended station at Glasbury-on-Wye in 1950. Glasbury was the last Midland station before Three Cocks Junction.
L&GRP (24929)

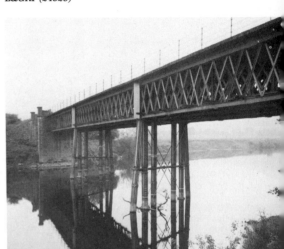

Above:
The small timber station building at Eardisley, seen in 1965 after the track had been lifted. *Chris Leigh*

Below:
A wealth of detail for the modeller can be seen in this illustration of Eardisley on 19 August 1964, in the last year of use. Collett 0-6-0 No 2242 shunts the goods depot. By now the line had been closed beyond this point (through passenger services having ceased on 31 December 1962) and Eardisley acted as the railhead for the remaining freight-only section. *B. J. Ashworth*

Ballabeg

Below:
John Cox's Ballabeg layout, based on the diminutive Isle of Man halt, was featured in the September 1985 *MRC*.

Here we feature four more views of this picturesque OOn12 layout which uses a number of the obsolete GEM kits. *Photographs: John Cox*

M. Arscott

'9F' with a difference

The '9F' class was perhaps the most successful of all the BR Standard designs, and their massive appearance with a multitude of wheels always suggested immense strength. Much has already been written about their outstanding performance, their short life (5-14 years), their success, and their popularity.

Back in the 1960s, when I was still at school, I had built for me a '9F' chassis; the idea being that I would put this under the body of the Kitmaster *Evening Star* plastic kit. These kits were excellent products and value for money, but possibly they were too cheap, for the firm collapsed and when Airfix acquired the moulds, many of the kits were never produced again.

Below:
The completed chassis with the Portescap motor/gearbox in place. *Author*

For many years my '9F' was the pride of my layout and performed well — in fact it still does! The brass-framed five-axle chassis has the drive on the fourth axle via a 40:1 worm and an MW5 motor, the bulk of which is situated in the firebox with the back of the magnet protruding into the cab.

Some years later Hornby Railways produced their version of the '9F' and at that time I was in a fortunate position to try out several different models, but was a little saddened to find that they were tender-driven with a somewhat disappointing performance.

Last year, more for curiosity than anything else, I purchased a Bristol Models chassis thinking I might be able to do a quick construction job using a super-detailed Airfix body. I found that the chassis, in milled brass, was very much of a scale effort and so the idea of the quick construction job disappeared. The

diameter of the driving wheels is 5ft and the chassis was already drilled at 5ft 5in centres (21.66mm) so using the recommended Romford 20m wheels which are actually over the flanges a generous 5ft 7in (22mm) presents a problem! I could, of course, have used 19mm wheels, but since the centre pair was to be flangeless as on the prototype, that only left the clearance problem between axles 1 & 2 and 4 & 5. I decided to turn a little off each flange, down to 21mm. So using an old Romford axle I mounted the four wheels in turn in the electric drill and, with a fine file, took a little off — down to the 21mm which then gave me ½mm clearance. That was the first problem solved!

I also became keen on the idea of a compensated chassis, with so many axles and my poor trackwork (I suspect I am not alone in this latter point), I kept wondering just how many wheels would be in contact with the rails at any one time and needless to say this goes hand-in-hand with electrical pick-up. Soon we are back to the beautiful exhibition locomotive, which only performs in fits and starts at all the demonstrations. I had in mind to use the Bristol Models chassis, Hornby valve gear, Airfix body and MTK 'BR1B' tender kit, and the excellent Kean-Portescap motor/gearbox. The final result however, was only vaguely along these lines as I will now reveal . . .

As my 'bread and butter' is earnt at sea, it is not possible to make quick trips to the local model shop, or to get damaged parts replaced quickly. In the process of joining my ship recently, our national airline, in typical fashion, 'mislaid' my suitcase. When it finally caught up with me some days later, it had obviously received 'special' treatment! A large tin of Humbrol matt black had burst, and apart from the general mess, most of it had given the unbuilt Airfix *Evening Star* kit a liberal coating! Some days later, those parts which had received most of the paint, started disintegrating all on their own.

Now the main part of the chassis is, as I've said, in milled brass, but the front chassis extensions are in white metal, which is a pity, since the cylinders hang on these and take a fair amount of pounding during construction. I prefer soldered construction to epoxy resin, so using the whitemetal bits as a pattern, I cut out new chassis extensions in nickel-silver, using the system of cutting out one frame first, then tack soldering it on to the other piece of nickel-silver and cutting round it, finally drilling the holes for the chassis spacers. This way both extensions and all the holes are equal — so of course are any mistakes! Using the spacer holes, I bolted both frames together (without the spacers) for a final check that they were both equal. All being well I then assembled the frames with the spacers.

While the frames were still together I also marked out the mid-points between axles 1 & 2 and 4 & 5, then scribed a line ⅛in above the centreline of all the axles and through the mid-points. This is the point at which the balance beams (for the two sets of floating axles) pivot, and I drilled a pilot hole with a No 75 drill. I next cut four strips 29mm long and 7mm wide out of some 20thou nickel-silver, which I find easier to work than the heavy chassis brass. Having marked out the centre, which is the mid-point distance of axles 1 & 2 and on the other two strips the mid-point of axles 4 & 5 I then marked out and drilled the axle centres, and inserted and soldered the brass bearings. I then enlarged the axle holes on the main frames — not the centre axle — by ½mm at the top and bottom, this governs the limit of the float or movement of the axles. The next stage was to cut two pieces of tube 1mm inside diameter by 7½mm long — this length depends on the thickness of the material used for making the balance beams. This tube and the rod to go through it, is usually available in aero model shops, and is used for their controls. One will have less problem if it is in brass and not steel or aluminium as these do not solder very well. I always carry two sizes with me — 1mm and 1.5mm, since the smaller makes a good valve rod and liner while the larger size is OK for a piston rod and liner, but more of that later. The next step was to assemble the beams, inserting the 1mm rod through the frame, the beam, the tube, the beam and the frame. If the second beam has to be forced too much then carefully (very carefully) with a fine file, take a little off the tube and try again until it is correct. Remember that a nice fit is required in which the beams float easily but do not slop about on their own. If you overdo this then the axles may develop horizontal play instead of just vertical, so patience is required. It is also better if the original hole, drilled No 75, is a fairly tight fit for the rod as this will remove the need for soldering, thus still allowing easy dismantling if ever required. Then insert all the wheels and axles and try on a piece of track and a point, to ensure that the axles are all floating easily with the undulations and that the wheels all rotate freely. If the floating action is still a little tight, dismantle and take just a little more off the tube which keeps the beams apart.

Care, patience, a little precision and a multitude of dry runs, will yield rewarding results. Always try to think at least two stages ahead in construction. If the patience wears

thin, put it aside for a day or so until you are in the right mood, but think of the problems and the ways round it. This sort of construction is not a 'Sunday afternoon-before-tea' job!

To aid the construction work I had taken with me only two books on the '9F's (always the wrong ones in retrospect) — *Locomotive Profile No 33* and *Locomotives Illustrated*. The former has several useful photos of chassis in various stages of construction; from these the next problem became apparent — all steam locomotive chassis look a bit bare in their lower regions without the brake blocks. On the prototype the hangers are between the wheels, but clearance is much too tight for this, so to hang them upwards in their correct position was the only feasible way that I could see around this one. Out of nickel-silver I made 10 extension brackets 2mm deep and drilled them with a No 75 drill. They were soldered mid-point between each axle, together with two extra length ones for the front wheels. The last pair should be to secure the rods, but turned out to be only for decoration since they are fitted below the rear of the cab. The brake blocks that I used were the MTK plastic ones. Fitting these was one of the very last jobs, but it is necessary to drill new holes and remove the moulded lugs. Being plastic there are no short circuit problems.

It is now time to think about the cylinders and valve gear, and to plan where and how to hang the cylinders. Both the Bristol Models white metal extensions and the Airfix frames use blocks and just glue the cylinder cover over the tops. Now, when I originally marked out the nickel-silver extensions, I also marked out the exact centre of the blocks and had drilled a

No 75 pilot hole. The cylinders, as supplied with this model, are white metal and just slide over the block on the same principle as Airfix! I decided to vary this slightly. So from nickel-silver I cut out a strip to the same dimensions as the back and ends of the box, drilled mid-point and bent to form a 'U' shape. The bottom of the 'U' screws via the pilot hole, into the frame. Across the open end I made four grooves. The two top ones were to recess partly a piece of 1mm tube and the two bottom ones to do the same for 1.5mm tube. This lower one can be soldered flush at the front and about 3mm protruding from the rear. Whichever cylinder casing one uses, it should slide neatly over this; the protrusion at the rear is only for decoration and on to it I fitted a small washer to represent the packing gland. Since I used the Bristol Models cover I drilled through the steamchest to take the 1mm tubing which protruded 2mm at the front and the same at the rear. I then adjusted the angle of the cylinders and soldered to the frame. When this operation is complete, it releases the unnecessary chassis spacer.

Both tubes, top and bottom, should be not less than 6mm away from the frames, and when making the grooves this can be checked on a dry fitting run. Any less than this and there are severe problems with coupling/connecting/wheel clearances. The 6mm is tight but quite workable. However, all sideplay must be taken out of the No 1 wheels by packing washers. I made an oversized one from scrap nickel-silver which more than covered the elongated axle

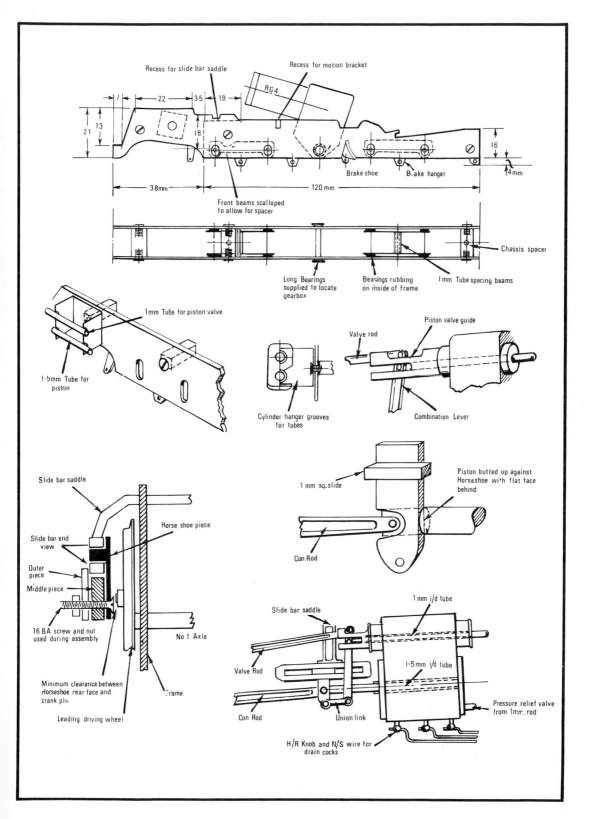

Recess for slide bar saddle

Recess for motion bracket

RG 4

7 22 3·5 19

21 13

18

Brake shoe

Brake hanger

16

14mm

38mm

120 mm

Front beams scalloped
to allow for spacer

Chassis spacer

Long Bearings
supplied to locate
gearbox

Bearings rubbing
on inside of frame

1mm Tube spacing beams

1mm Tube for piston valve

1·5mm Tube for
piston

Cylinder hanger grooves
for tubes

Piston valve guide

Valve rod

Combination Lever

Slide bar saddle

Horse shoe piece

Slide bar end
view

Outer
piece

Middle piece

16 BA screw and nut
used during assembly

No 1 Axle

Minimum clearance between
Horseshoe rear face and
crank pin

Frame

Leading driving wheel

1 mm sq. slide

Piston butted up against
Horseshoe with flat face
behind

Con Rod

Slide bar saddle

1 mm i/d tube

Valve Rod

1·5mm i/d tube

Con Rod

Union link

Pressure relief valve
from 1mm rod

H/R Knob and N/S wire for
drain cocks

hole, and a smaller packing washer on either side. Remember, the axle must still float freely, but without any sideplay.

On the rear of the top tube I made yet another 'U' shape. This time both sides were 7mm long, the bottom of the 'U' 4mm, and all were 3mm wide. I cut a slot either end and, of course, made a pilot hole for the centre, which was then opened out to fit over the protruding rear of the top tube. This forms a guide for the piston valve and valve rod coupling. (Note that the Airfix and Hornby models are non-working dummies.) At this stage the only parts permanently soldered should be the cylinders, casing and brake hangers. Anything else should be only tack-soldered so that it can be moved for adjustment.

The slidebars are not attached to the cylinders but instead are hung from a 'saddle' over the frames. In my box of metal bits I found some 3mm 'U' shaped channel which appeared to be a fair representation of the prototype. The slidebars themselves were made from 1mm square nickel-silver. I formed one piece so that I would only have to solder one end and the gap in the middle was exactly 1mm. This job is not as bad as it sounds, although it requires patience. I then chamfered off the bottom and top rear ends. I found the former to be very necessary if the connecting rod was to clear it. The next stage was a bit of trial and error to find

out the length and the angle of the saddle for the slidebars. The slidebar wants to be exactly over the top of the piston rod with more of a tendency to be outside this centre line than inside. The length is found by measuring the length of the stroke, ascertained by revolving the centre wheel with the connecting rod hung on, from full forward to full back, or twice the distance from the centre of the axle to the crankpin, plus ½mm for clearance. This is a bit of a 'chicken and egg' situation and I made the piston and slidebars at the same time. The piston is made from three pieces soldered one on top of the other. The first part is shaped like a horseshoe but with a square front and extra thick sides. The left, or top, will extend 3mm up behind the slidebar and will have soldered on to it a piece 1mm square, which slides between the slidebars. The lower, or right hand side, tapers or is rounded off near the bottom and has a No 75 hole drilled ½mm from the bottom (for the union link). Over that was a piece with same dimensions but no cut out as in the horseshoe, which is incidentally to accommodate the leading end of the connecting rod. The upper surface of this slides along the lower surface of the lower slide bar. Next (do not solder this yet) is a piece of the same but 1mm longer than the last fitted from between the frame and the slidebar. All this is done without the wheels in position as there is more space to work. Before shaping all these bits, I drilled a No 75 pilot hole through the lower part, which will eventually hold the back end of the union link. From this hole I measured 3mm back and drilled again. This would be the hole through which the con-rod is attached and from here to the lower slidebar is 1.75mm. All this makes the horseshoe 8mm and the middle piece of a length of 5mm. The extra ½mm is below the union link hole and the width is 4mm. Having made these bits, I put a 16BA screw through the union link hole and added a nut which is sufficient just to hold the assembly. In order to attach the piston rod to this lot, I carefully filed a flat 4mm long on to a piece of 1.5mm rod and then butted the rod end of the flat up against the horseshoe and soldered. By carefully drilling through the middle piece and horseshoe con-rod hole, it should come through the middle of this flat. This then forms the other side of the middle piece, preventing the con rod from falling out of the horseshoe. All the pilot holes are drilled out with a No 75 drill as this is just the size for normal nickel-silver handrail wire. A piece of this through the horseshoe will secure the con-rod without having to solder anything.

We should by now have a piston rod attached to its slide and able to move between the slidebars. The important thing is the correct distance between the piston rod and the slide, which is now permanently soldered to the horseshoe, because this is the distance at which the slidebars must hang at this stage it is far easier to adjust the height of the slidebars.

Having looked closely at the Hornby valve-gear it would, of course, be a lot easier to fit, but it is a little crude and since I had already spent a great deal of time and effort with the chassis, I decided to use an Eames/Jamieson valve gear kit (LNER pattern).

The next stage was to make up the valve gear. I first made the valve rod, from 1mm diameter rod, and made a small L-shaped piece. This I drilled on one side to take the 1mm rod, soldering this straight away. Then on the other arm of the 'L' I drilled again with No 75. The next job was to find the length of the combination lever. I drilled the two top holes No 75 and inserted two pieces of nickel-silver wire, the lower one through the piston valve (L-shape) and the top one which will eventually hold the valve rod. Now, with the centre wheel at bottom dead centre, the piston slide should be exactly half-way along the slide bars and the union link facing forward should cross the combination lever at right angles. Where they cross is the point to drill through. To do this I also made a small washer and drilled it to fit between the outer cover of the horseshoe and the union link. It gives just that little bit more clearance between the combination lever and the slidebars, and can temporarily be held tight for measurement by the 16BA nut and screw. Now if you are going to use Jamieson rivets for the valve gear it requires a No 56 drill. For many years I was hopeless at this task and found it far easier with a No 75, N/S wire and a small washer for the other end. If using this method, use a small soldering iron (around 15W) and always place a piece of paper between the work and the washer (as if it was a paper washer). That way you can push the N/S or brass washer right home with the end of a small file without the fear of welding the whole lot solid. When in place, pull out the paper and the link should rotate quite freely. The other end of the wire was first soldered (usually to the inside) to the inner link to be joined. Attach the valve rod to the top hole of the combination lever and the other end to the expansion link, which is attached to, and pivots in the motion bracket, the construction of which I'll come to in a second.

Normally on models this valve rod is set in 'mid-gear' position on the expansion link and thus does not move very much. Just to be different, I dropped the link right to the bottom of the expansion link and put it therefore in Full Forward gear. This is far more impressive to observers, since there is now a lot more action out of both the valve rod and combination lever (it's also a bit more fiddly to do, but if you're still with me, then I'm sure you can work that bit out).

Now to the motion bracket. The choice is yours. Both the Hornby and the Airfix ones are only very rough approximations, but still sticking to the principle that 'I've got this far so why spoil it now', I pressed on, and here I really could have wished that I had a better selection of books. I started with the left-hand or driver's side and this bears a resemblance to the Airfix moulding. It is difficult to explain since it is very much a three dimensional piece. It is like a box with a partition in it but without a back or an end on the out facing side. Through the open side of the box, through the piece facing forward is a bell crank, from the front of which hangs a short reversing link attached to the valve rod. If lifted, it moves the valve rod up or down the crescent-shaped expansion link, moving the valve rod forward or backward thus changing the position of the valves in the steam chest. The other end of the bell crank is attached to a worm and gear, which in turn is attached to the long reversing rod that goes back into the cab.

Below:
Cabside and piping details of '9F' 2-10-0 No 92234 at Banbury in 1966.

The back of the box to the mid-partition is made from one shaped strip of 20 thou right across the frames to the other motion bracket and slotted into the frames. The exact dimensions of the box are now difficult to gauge, but I made it by relating the size to other known

parts. The motion bracket proper I made from a piece of 3mm channel bent over backwards to form a 'U' shape (it is necesary to make two cuts in each piece of the channel corner) and drilled No 75 to take the pivot for the expansion link.

The fireman's side/right-hand motion bracket is a far simpler affair and nothing like the Airfix version. From the motion bracket (across the frames) hangs another piece of 3mm channel with a bend in it and a lightening hole in the channel. Now either make another U-shaped channel to take the expansion link (as on the left) bend as required, (just solder to the end of the channel) or solder a piece to the back of the channel thus forming a 'U' shape that way and drill as usual through the bottom.

I should perhaps mention that the Bristol Models chassis is already milled out to take an XO4/MW5 or Romford Bulldog motor and would drive the fourth axle. However since this axle is now floating, that type of motor is definitely out. If you have never tried a Portescap motor/gearbox then you have a treat in store; no more meshing gears, for a start, and no more choosing gear ratios. The Portescap just drops between the frames and the axle is pushed through the middle. The gear wheel is supplied and so are the axle bushes. The gear ratio is a standard 38:1. On the '9F' with 5ft wheels this gives a scale top speed of about 90mph and a scale minimum of about ½mph and the latter has to be seen to be believed.

Assuming that you are still with me, that completes the bulk of the chassis except for one novelty feature, and that is the working linkage of the mechanical lubricator. This really was quite a challenge! At first I made the rod a fixture, but after a little thought, decided that I could get it to work. Although the rods are small they are quite a prominent feature of the Standard locomotives. A piece of 1.5mm by 1mm and 40mm long nickel silver (heavier slide bar material) was soldered in a gentle 'V' shape on top of the slide bar saddle with both ends turned down vertically and drilled No 75. A piece of nickel silver wire, 10mm long, with the ends turned in opposite directions (like a 'Z') goes through one of the holes in the 'V' shape which represents the lubricator and is hidden by the running plate, (hence the 'V' shape is sufficient). I soldered a narrow piece of nickel-silver along the back of what was to be the lower link and through one end of this flat which overlaps the end by about ½mm. Drilled No 75, this would take the unattached end of the link from the lubricator. Now, to produce a miniature link which is clamped to the expansion link pivot is really stretching things a bit too far but by carefully bending this end of

the rod inwards at 90°, drilling No 75 through the valve rod and then soldering a small dummy piece extending the lower link back to just under the expansion pivot, as the valve rod moves, so does the lubricator linkage.

The only remaining task of any real importance is to construct the coupling rods; and the geometry here really has to be accurate. There are eight rods to be made. Ideally they should have been made at the same time as the balance beams. The rods are of the plain 'fish bellied' type, and since the axles are now floating, they must all be individual. Make each rod separately and make the holes by finding (I used a pair of dividers) the exact axle centres. This point cannot be too highly stressed. The one trick I did learn was that if the holes are slightly elongated and a washer the exact size of the crankpin is used and soldered over the elongated hole then in position on the crankpin, careful use of the iron will allow them to be moved the merest fraction (the washers also form well-shaped oil boxes). The hardest problem is finding which hole is actually out of alignment.

I now fitted the brake blocks. I then coupled up the connecting rods and return cranks with spacers between them, and set the cranks at about 10° before centre. Since the nickel silver rod for the brakes goes right through the frames, I used these to hang two pieces of copper-clad paxolin to which the nickel-silver pick-ups were soldered.

For detail, I added the cylinder drain cocks (three handrail knobs each side) and a pressure relief valve at the bottom front of each piston. I soldered the buffer beam on to the front chassis extensions and soldered on the sprung buffers, the sprung Jackson screw coupling and my own bar type coupling without the hook. On the fireman's side the most noticeable thing must surely be the mass of copper pipes for the injectors; here again the Airfix and the Hornby versions are only rough approximations. I made a new pair and soldered them to the frames with a piece of small brass angle. I had been using the Airfix footplate but the cab sides had suffered badly at the hands of the airline and the footplate had split. I patched the footplate but was still unhappy about it. Using the plastic parts as patterns I cut new cab sides and a cab roof from 20 thou nickel-silver sheet. I added window frames and ribbing from brass wire, and the cab roof ventilator from scrap brass off the edge of an etched kit (I never throw this surplus metal away).

At about this time I had just finished reading part of *Firing Days at Saltley* by Terry Essery and had quite entered into the spirit of the

Above:
Tender rear details of BR1C tender on a '9F' at Stoke in 1967. *C. Tanous*

'Nines'. I had already decided to be different and make it a single chimney version which also had the footplate under the smokebox door as opposed to the small steps. It would also have a 'BR1C' type tender. Fortunately for me the two boiler halves and smokebox door had escaped the airline's destruction attempt. I am really very poor at making boilers and fireboxes and was determined to avoid this if possible. Now there is nothing to my mind that looks worse than plastic piping moulded on to a boiler. Whichever way it is painted, it still looks plastic, and so carefully using a sharp scalpel, I cut off all the piping and handrails and cleaned up the boiler with a file, redrilling holes for the handrail knobs as I went. Meanwhile I was still thinking about the footplate and attaching new metal footsteps and lamp brackets etc. Finally, it started to disintegrate in my hands. So that was it, now a new footplate was cut in one piece with the valancing soldered on after bending to shape; all out of 20thou nickel silver sheet. I made new sandbox fillers out of scrap copper wire and an offcut of 3mm brass channel (even the little bits come in handy). The strength at the rear of the footplate was regained when I soldered the cab in place and soldered on new brass angle for steps up the side of the

deflectors. I made a new steam manifold out of heavy brass as the Airfix one had collapsed. I was determined to use the ash pan from the Airfix kit, so I cut it out and it just fell apart. The ashpan was an awkward shape to make but it looks all right now. All the pipework was replaced and the cab windows glazed (using clear thick Plastruct). The pipework is all out of various bits of old scrap electrical cable. The footplate steps are from 20 thou brass angle. I then turned my attention to making a new cab interior. This is based on the Airfix parts and a photograph in *Loco Profile* of a stoker-fitted '9F'. The dials and gauges are chopped off pieces of 8 and 10 screws and all the rest is from brass or copper wire and scrap fret; the reversing wheel is a washer with its fret tab left on and bent over to represent the handle. The draught screens at both side windows are again brass wire and 'Devconned' on to a slither of blister pack! The tender started life as an MTK 'BR1B'. Fortunately in my earlier years I had made it with epoxy resin and it came to pieces easily. I might perhaps have left it, but it also had suffered from flying and the non-pinpoint axles were very tight to turn. So, I made a new tender subframe altogether, which did not use the white metal axleboxes at all, but now just run on the N/S frames. Used 'BIC' ball-point centre ink containers are conveniently the same size as the axles so slices of tube form instant spacers to prevent wheels shorting on the chassis and also remove some of the sideplay from the axles. The original white metal rear ladder was replaced by a piece of signal ladder.

Looking through the various books that I had with me I found an abundance of photographs with tenders almost totally bereft of coal, and remembering some of Terry Essery's experiences on trips to Carlisle, I decided yet again, to be different. I had to construct a hopper-type coal box, a fire iron tunnel, and the recessed tender doors on to the footplate. The hopper construction was relatively simple using scrap brass fret. The tender front replacement was another story. The original MTK one was a sort of approximation, while the Airfix one, which I might have been tempted to use, was for the 'BR1G' tender with the inset coalbox and was slightly different. So with a photograph of the stoker-fitted tender front, I built a new front. It was made in two pieces, a front and a back spaced apart by two pieces of heavy chassis brass (which was tough to cut) especially as they had to line up with the recessed doors and form the lockers and the two ledges either side. The brake and water scoop handles are from brass wire set in a No 75 hole! The locker doors and shovelling plate are scrap brass fret again. The fall plate works as on the prototype, the hinge being a piece of nickel silver half-round wire, the ends of which are the two handrail plates either side (scrap brass of course). The tender doors are paper 'Devconned' to the handrail plates and painted black. The lower footplate top and front are from nickel silver. The dome and the rear section of the tender top are also the original MTK white metal parts. This last part is perhaps a bit gimmicky but gave me enjoyment proving a point to myself. The last photograph in *Locomotive Illustrated* shows 92019 heading north with a Long Meg anhydrate train. The view shows the rear of the 'BR1C' well, and also the fact that the tank lid had not been closed after filling with water. A piece of nickel silver, a circle of nickel silver wire, and a piece of brass (for the hinge) small file, and solder and we have just reproduced the heavy round tank lid that opens and closes on a 'BR1C' tender!

With all 10 driving wheels firmly on the track, the haulage power was quite incredible but I now have added small chopped up pieces of lead and solder and scrap white metal in the firebox and smokebox, and the haulage powers have now increased dramatically again.

I hope that I can now get this back to the UK without any more subversion from airlines; I also hope that this article has not put you off. The joy of this for me has to be the achievement in producing what I thought was beyond my talents and in overcoming the various problems — plus some pleasant hours running when I get back to the UK.

Below:
BR Standard '9F' 2-10-0 No 92154 at Cricklewood on 30 December 1963. *R. Wildsmith*

Stanley C. Jenkins

East Gloucestershire Railway Stations

The architecture of the GWR can be divided into two historical groups, ie 'Early Victorian' and 'Standard' (see p134, May 1974 *Railway Modeller*). There is, however, a large sub-grouping of stations which do not fit this rigid pattern, and these are the branch line stations. The reason for this is simple: a few of the branch lines of the GWR were actually built by the Great Western Railway Co; most were constructed by small, local concerns which after a few years of independent existence sold out to the Great Western. It follows, therefore, that the architecture of these minor companies will be completely non-standard. In fact, when one is modelling a Great Western branch line, almost anything goes. Indeed, I would go so far as to suggest that, unless a particular absorbed station has been rebuilt by the GWR, it is not a Great Western station at all! It will continue to reflect the character of the original company.

Obviously, it would be impossible to describe the architecture of every Great Western branch line in a short article such as this. What I can do, however, is to present the plans of one company's architectural style — the East Gloucestershire Railway, and at the same time mention some of the other designs for which plans, photographs, or other details have been published.

I have chosen the East Gloucestershire Railway for the simple reason that no plans of

Below:
A general view of Fairford station with its interesting mixture of original East Gloucestershire Railway buildings and later GWR structures. The station building and goods shed in local stone have been supplemented with GWR sheds of various types, while the signalbox is a modified standard type with the back wall angled to allow access to the loading dock. *Real Photographs*

its intermediate stations have been published. Moreover, the design is a simple one that could well form the basis of a first attempt at scratch-building.

The EGR was a very rural line, really nothing but an extension of the earlier Witney Railway. Running for 14 miles through flat, upper Thames Valley countryside, the line terminated in a meadow about a mile from the town of Fairford. (It had originally been intended to take the line through to Cheltenham, but the

Above:
A closer view of the signalbox and goods shed on 23 May 1962, with '74XX' 0-6-0PT No 7404 between duties. Note the slatted doors to the goods shed. *Ian Allan Library*

Below:
The angled rear corner of the signalbox is clearly seen in this view, looking east on 9 April 1960. *F. Hornby*

EGR could not afford to do this, and the GWR could hardly be expected to lend the money to a potential rival). The EGR and the Witney

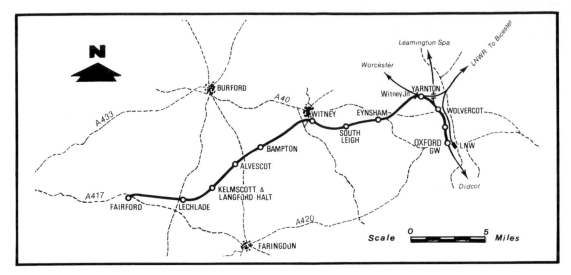

Railway had been worked by the GWR since their opening (the Witney Railway had been opened in 1861, and the EGR followed in 1873). Both companies were fully absorbed by the GWR in 1890, and settled down to a sleepy existence as a branch line. The Fairford branch as we can now call it, joined the Oxford-Worcester line at Yarnton Junction, and the branch trains ran down the main line for three miles to Oxford, where (if one was lucky), they connected with the Paddington expresses. The line lost its passenger services in 1962, and the former section was closed completely. The

Witney Railway lingered on as a freight-only line until 1970.

So much for the history of the line. If any readers wish to know more, there are several accounts available (see the bibliography below). Typically, however, these accounts ignore the architecture of the railway completely, and are

Below:
Lechlade station building was almost identical to Fairford and the general site layout was also very similar. On 5 July 1958 0-6-0PT No 7411 arrives at Lechlade with a down train. *E. Wilmshurst*

Above:

Standard GWR lamps, nameboard and 'pagoda' cycle shed adorn the platform at Lechlade as No 7404 waits with the branch brake van on 30 May 1962. *Ian Allan Library*

therefore of limited use to the modeller. Hence it is perhaps justifiable to attempt to redress the balance.

As will be seen from the illustrations, the EGR had a distinct architectural style, which is clearly influenced by the use of local materials and local traditions. The stations at Fairford, Lechlade, Alvescot and Bampton were all built to this design. For some inexplicable reason, Alvescot station was constructed of brick, while the other stations were stone-built. There was also an East Gloucestershire station at Witney. The layout of this building was different to that of the smaller stations. There was a small canopy and an extension on the road side of the building. These are almost certainly later additions, the extension being in quite a different style, while the timber-framed canopy is a free-standing structure.

Fairford station has recently been taken over and rebuilt to form the offices of a farm distribution firm, while Lechlade, Alvescot and Witney have been demolished. Only Bampton remains in something approaching its original condition.

Obviously, the original design has been altered at Bampton; the eastern end has been extended to produce an enlarged parcels office. The arrangement of the chimneys has also been changed. The original chimney on the western end has been replaced by a tall single flue stack at the rear of the building, serving the office, and a stove-pipe from the new parcels office. A retired stone-mason, Mr W. J. Lock, told me that these alterations were carried out sometime after World War 1, by a contractor from Witney. I am not sure if the appearance of the building was improved or not. Certainly, the symmetry of the design has been lost, but on the other hand the unmatching gable ends and the new chimneys give the building a certain character, which is perhaps missing in the original design. However, readers can judge for themselves.

I have deliberately omitted details of the track plans, cycle sheds, signals, etc of the EGR stations. I am merely concerned here with the architecture of the company — railway architecture being a particularly neglected aspect of our hobby. If anyone should decide to model the EGR or any other company, then he must surely embark on his own research, and not rely entirely on secondary sources! If, however, I have managed to show that there is more to modelling station buildings than erecting a few kits, then I will be content! Kit-built structures do have their place though, especially if one is modelling an imaginary GW branch line — in this case it could be argued that the stations are relics of the line's original ownership. I would suggest, tentatively, that the two Bilteezi station kits have the best GW branch-line atmosphere. The Superquick and former Airfix kits, on the other hand seem better suited to a main line or suburban layout.

On a Great Western branch line then, there is tremendous scope for the design of the station buildings; kit-built structures, freelance designs, prototype models. There is room for

Above:
Lechlade yard and standard EGR goods shed on 30 May 1962. *Ian Allan Library*

them all. However, since so many prototype stations have been destroyed in recent years, I feel that there is a special attraction in prototype-based models.

BIBLIOGRAPHY OF ARTICLES ON THE FAIRFORD BRANCH:

The Oxford, Witney & Fairford Railway by C. L. Mowat p191, March 1931 *Railway Magazine.*

The Oxford, Witney & Fairford Line by T. J. Saunders p677, October 1960 *Railway Magazine.*

Fairwell to the Fairford Branch by J. M. Tolson p337, October 1962 *Railway World.*

The Story of Witney's Railways by D. A. E. Cross (published in the *Witney Gazette* between 21 January and 23 February 1966).

Also *The Fairford Branch* (Branch Line Handbooks), *Great Western Branch Line Termini* (OPC), *GWR Country Stations Vols 1 & 2* (Ian Allan Ltd).

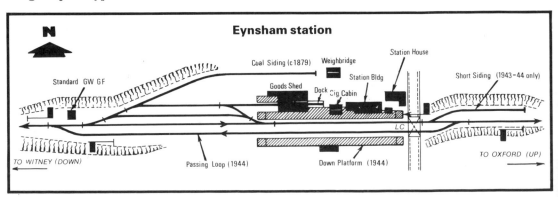

Witney Station

Opened by the East Gloucestershire Railway on 14 January 1873, Witney passenger station consisted of a passing loop, with up and down platforms. The main station buildings were on the up platform, and there was a small waiting shelter on the down side. No goods facilities were provided, and goods trains had to reverse into the nearby ex-Witney Railway station, which became Witney goods yard on the opening of the East Gloucestershire extension. (Later, however, a small end-loading dock was added at the

Above:
With the opening of the EGR and Witney (new) station, the original Witney Railway terminus became the goods yard. The original station building seen here served as offices with 'WITNEY GOODS DEPOT' on a brown and cream enamelled British Railways sign below the eaves. Since goods services outlasted the passenger trains by some 10 years, this building actually outlived the newer and more substantial EGR station.

Below:
'74XX' 0-6-0PT No 7404 arrives at Witney with a down train formed of one coach and a van on 30 May 1962. The old station is hidden behind the 'pagoda' shed.
Ian Allan Library

passenger station and this was occasionally used to load and unload road vehicles, machinery and horses.)

The station building originally consisted of a simple rectangular structure, with half-hipped gables at each end; in this form it resembled the other stations on the East Gloucestershire Railway such as Bampton and Fairford. Old photographs show that Witney station had a small canopy which extended for roughly three fifths of the way along the platform side, covering the doors leading to the ladies and waiting rooms. The parcels office, at the west end of the building,

Top:
Witney (new) station from the approach road, showing the hip-roofed extension on this side of the building.
Ian Allan Library

Above:
'2251' 0-6-0 No 2221, a regular Fairford branch locomotive, leaves the terminus on 28 May 1962. *Ian Allan Library*

was uncovered[1]. This canopy was later extended westwards and given a much deeper valance, with typical Great Western 'V and Hole' decoration. Scarf joints were used to unite the old and new sections of framework and when the work was finished

Above:
No 7404 shunts the yard at Fairford on 23 May 1962. The EGR goods shed can be seen in the background. Note the unusual method of shunting!
Ian Allan Library

Below:
At the extreme end of the branch, well beyond the station, stood Fairford's locomotive facilities. The turntable, water tank and locomotive shed are here seen shortly before closure. *Ian Allan Library*

it was hard to see the actual joins — the only clue being the rather odd spacing of the support posts! The date of this alteration is not clear but it is thought that the work was relatively modern, possibly c1920.

Other alterations carried out at around this time resulted in the complete rebuilding of the structure. An extension at the rear enabled the parcels and booking offices to be enlarged and a new waiting room was added at the back — the old waiting room then became part of the booking office. The double

doors that had hitherto opened on to the platform were made into a window, and as the newly enlarged booking office was rather dark, a skylight was let into the roof.

Witney passenger station was closed to passengers on 16 June 1962, but remained in full use until May 1965; amusingly, it was still possible to book tickets from the station — although of course one could no longer travel. The withdrawal of parcels and sundries traffic in 1966 resulted in complete closure of Witney passenger station and the building was demolished in January 1969. Only the platforms now remain.

The main details will be fairly clear from the above notes, but there are one or two further points which could be made. Window and door apertures tended to be of varying dimensions — this being the result of the rather complicated changes outlined above. The position of a western chimney stack was marked by new ridge tiles, which did not match their neighbours. This chimney origi-

Above:
No 2221 at Witney station with an up train running 'wrong line'. This was normal practice when the up platform was obstructed with vans being loaded. The waiting shelter and lamps on the down platform can be seen. *Ian Allan Library*

Right:
A splendid gas lamp and the details of the down platform timber waiting shelter are visible in this view of No 3653 at Witney with a down train. *Ian Allan Library*

nally served fireplaces in the parcels and booking offices. Similarly, the eastern chimney contained two flues, one from the Ladies Room, the other from the old Waiting Room (the latter was blocked up during the alterations).

The walls were constructed of coursed rubble, with ashlar dressings. Roof tiles were

Above:
Witney goods yard also sported a large goods shed of GWR origin and fairly standard design. It is seen in this view of No 7404 shunting the yard on 30 May 1962.
Ian Allan Library

reddish-orange. The early colour scheme is unknown, but there are indications that the East Gloucestershire Railway stations were painted in green and cream. In more recent times, GWR 'stone' paint colours predominated. In 1956 or thereabouts, the Western Region repainted the structure in brown and cream.

Such are the physical details of Witney passenger station — a station which was, until comparatively recent times, a centre of economic and social activity. Commodities handled at the passenger station included mail, small parcels, and milk; whilst over at the goods depot coal, stone, wool, blankets, grain, scrap metal and hay formed the bulk of the traffic. In 1933 (a typical year), some 49,059 tons of freight were moved to or from Witney[2]. There were around seven passenger trains each way daily, plus two freight workings and a cattle train on market days. The station gave employment to about 26 men, excluding those needed to operate the trains. Yet, the railway in those days was not merely a means of transport; it seems that, 40 years ago, the youth of the town used to meet in the waiting room — where, in the winter, there was a welcoming coal fire! In addition, the well-used chocolate machine, which yielded bars of chocolate in return for one (proper) penny, appears to have been a prime attraction!

In summer, the platforms were the setting for attractive floral displays — for, in those prewar years, the 'Best Kept Station' competition was a big event. (Lechlade was a major rival.) Finally, and still in retrospective vein, it may come as a surprise to learn that the station sold a variety of publications, including hefty, hard cover monographs such as *Castles*, *Abbeys* and *Cathedrals*; various County guides; jigsaws (!) and the well-remembered *Holiday Haunts*, an annual directory and gazeteer, which set out, county by county, the many delightful places linked, like Witney, to the Great Western Railway[3].

(1) See photograph on p24 of *The Witney & East Gloucestershire Railway* (Oakwood Press, 1975).

(2) On average, around 40,000 tons of freight were carried each year until 1965, when the goods department was run down.

(3) See R. B. Wilson, *Go Great Western*, for complete list of GW literature, surviving examples of these works are now much sought after.

Somersetshire Midland

Prototype and Model

Above:
The prototype is a standard Canadian Pacific structure used for drying and storing sand for locomotives. The sand is delivered to the ground level bunker, dried inside the shed and blown by compressed air into the upper silo, whence it is delivered by gravity down a flexible spout into the locomotive sandboxes. This example at Victoria in British Columbia is still used for diesel locomotives.
Chris Leigh

Left:
A model sand tower in HO scale built of balsa with card roof and metal pipework and based on a drawing by Jack Work, published in the USA some years ago.

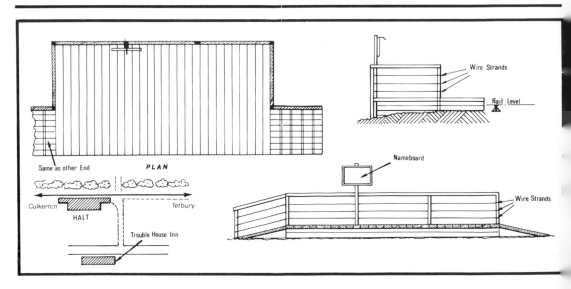

Chris Leigh

Troublehouse

During 1959 the Western Region introduced the first AC Cars diesel railbuses experimentally on the Kemble-Tetbury and Kemble-Cirencester branches. At the time the vehicles offered great potential, and a big drive was made to increase passenger traffic on the lines. Two new halts were built on each of the branches, and Culkerton station, which had been derelict for some years, was re-opened as an unstaffed halt.

The four new halts, at Troublehouse and Churchs Hill on the Tetbury branch, and Park Leaze and Chesterton Lane on the Cirencester line, were spartan affairs. They were designed to make use of the special folding steps fitted to the railbuses, and the platforms were only a few inches above rail height. They measured 28ft 6in by 15ft, and were built up from old sleepers, with the chair marks still visible.

No shelter was provided, the halt having a post and rail fence surrounding it, with a few strands of wire threaded between the posts. The nameboard was mounted on a single wooden post, the lettering being painted in cream on the chocolate brown-coloured board.

The drawings and illustration show Troublehouse Halt, which served the ancient public house of the same name. The design of the halts made boarding the train difficult for elderly people, so at Troublehouse a beer crate was utilised to provide a step up to the train.

The railbus experiments were said to have been unsuccessful, and in April 1964 the services on both branches were withdrawn. As freight services had already gone from the Tetbury branch, the track was lifted and the halts and Culkerton station were demolished. The Cirencester branch was lifted in 1966, leaving the town without a rail connection.

Bottom left:
Troublehouse halt: plan view, front and end elevations to 2mm scale.

Below:
Troublehouse halt on the Kemble-Tetbury branch on 29 August 1959. *M. G. Farr*

TRAVEL BY TGV FROM LYON TO PARIS – WIN A HOLIDAY FOR TWO IN FRANCE

How well do you know your motive power? How quickly could you tell a 'Jubilee' from a 'Black 5' or a rebuilt 'Royal Scot' from a rebuilt 'Patriot' as they raced towards you? On the modern scene can you spot the differences between a '47/3' and '47/4' or differentiate at 100 yards between a Class 81 and a Class 84 electric locomotive? Put your knowledge of the details of British motive power old and new to the test in this brain-teasing quiz. Simply read the rules below, fill in the official entry form and send it and the competition voucher (to be found at the front of the Annual) to IAN ALLAN LTD. In the event of a tie, the winners will be chosen by means of a draw.

PRIZES

- FIRST PRIZE (One winner)
  A LONG WEEKEND FOR TWO IN FRANCE, in association with BR and the French Travel Service. *Wednesday:* First class rail journey to Heathrow. Depart by air to Lyon. *Thursday:* A day in Lyon. *Friday:* By TGV to Paris. *Saturday:* A day in Paris. *Sunday:* Return flight to London; first-class rail return home.

- SECOND PRIZE (One winner)
  A SEVEN-DAY LOCAL ROVER TICKET of *your choice.*

- THIRD PRIZE (Five winners)
  A TWO-YEAR SUBSCRIPTION to the Ian Allan Ltd magazine of *your choice.*

RULES

1. Entries must be made on one of the official entry forms published in *Railway World, Modern Railways, Model Railway Constructor* and *Motive Power Monthly* in the August 1986, December 1986 and February 1987 issues and other Ian Allan Ltd rail magazines.

2. All entries must be accompanied by a competition voucher from one of the Ian Allan Ltd 1987 rail annuals *(Model Railway Constructor Annual 1987, Railway World Annual 1987, Motive Power Annual 1987).*

3. The judges' decision will be final.

4. No correspondence regarding this competition can be entered into.

5. No employee or his/her family of the Ian Allan Group of companies may enter this competition.

6. The closing date for this competition is 28 February 1987. Entries received after this date will not be accepted.

7. Prizewinners will be notified by post; all will also be announced in the May-dated issues of *Modern Railways, Railway World, Motive Power Monthly* and *Model Railway Constructor.*

Part 1: What Numbers?

Compiled by Colin J. Marsden

1. Which locomotive operated the Earl Mountbatten funeral train empty stock into Waterloo?

2. What number was carried by the first Class 455/7 unit when delivered?

3. Which Southern Region locomotive hauled the 'Gatwick Express' exhibition train in the North of England in early 1984?

4. Which locomotive was the last to retain original green livery?

5. Which locomotive was hauling the train involved in the 'Great Train Robbery'?

6. What was the number of the locomotive which a clairvoyant predicted would be involved in a serious accident, and what was it renumbered as?

7. What locomotive was involved in the Hixon level crossing collision?

8. Which Class 47 was experimentally fitted with Blue Star multiple control equipment?

9. Which was the first Class 50 to be refurbished?

10. Which Class 52 locomotive received the last classified overhaul at BREL Swindon?

Part 2: True or False?

1. The maximum permitted speed for High Speed Trains in passenger service is 155mph.

2. The Class 210 (DEMU), and Class 317 (EMU) can be operated in multiple.

3. Driverless operation on selected SR suburban lines will commence in 1987.

4. Only trains with barred windows can operate on the North London line due to the unruly behaviour of travellers.

5. Certain Mk 2 stock is fitted with subdued lighting for the benefit of tired passengers on overnight services.

6. The famous R&D Division at Derby is the base for Reckless & Disqualified drivers who are not permitted to operate passenger trains.

7. When operating normally in passenger service all trains must have a continuous brake pipe throughout the train.

8. A Class 50 locomotive has been used on the Glasgow-Edinburgh high speed service.

9. The Isle of Wight electric stock is regularly transferred by means of road and boat to BREL Eastleigh for classified attention.

10. Although the maximum permitted speed for the Class 27 is 90mph, when operating with 100mph stock they may operate at the higher speed.

Part 3: Steam Locomotives *Compiled by Brian Morrison*

How well do you know your motive power? Put your knowledge of the details of British motive power old and new to the test in this brain-teasing quiz. Can you identify the steam locomotives shown here?

1

2

5

4

6

7

8

9

10

13

12

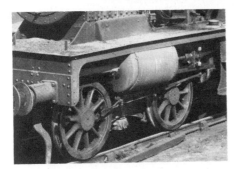

14

15

16

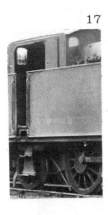

17

18

19

20

Part 4: Modern Traction

Compiled by Colin J. Marsden

1. What class of locomotive was this?

2. What three numbers did this locomotive carry?

3. On which Region do these units operate, and to what class/sub-class do they belong?

4. Which class of locomotive was this originally, and what was its later classification and use?

5. What class and sub-class does this locomotive conform to?

6. What class of locomotive was this, and what method of transmission was employed?

7. To which locomotive class and sub-class does this locomotive belong?

10

11

12

8. These air and electrical connections belong to which class/sub-class of locomotive?

9. What is this item of equipment and on which class of unit was it fitted?

10. To which locomotive did these air louvres belong, and what was its final number?

11. On which class of locomotive can this be found?

12. What is this, and on what locomotive class would it be found?

13

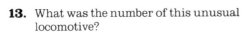

13. What was the number of this unusual locomotive?

14. On which class of diesel unit is this front end window layout to be found?

15. What locomotive class does this equipment come from?

15